D0268130

Glenveagh
National Park....

a remote and hauntingly beautiful wilderness

Aran
Island

GLENVEAGH
NATIONAL
PARK

Burt Castle

Derr

contents

Conversion Chart

Metric measurements are used throughout this book.
The imperial scale equivalents can be obtained from the chart below:

Height/distance:

Metric	Imperial
1 metre (m)	3.28 feet
100 metres (m)	109 yards
1 kilometre (km)	0.6214 mile (3 kilometres is just over 2 miles)

Area:

Metric	Imperial
1 hectare (ha)	2.47 acres

GLENVEAGH
NATIONAL
PARK

Aran
Island

Burt Castle

Der

Glenveagh National Park

Glenveagh National Park lies in the heart of the Derryveagh Mountains in the north-west of County Donegal. It is a remote and hauntingly beautiful wilderness of rugged mountains and pristine lakes. The Park, over 14,000 hectares in extent, consists of three areas. The largest of these is the former Glenveagh Estate, including most of the Derryveagh Mountains. To the west are the quartzite hills around Crocknafarragh and to the south, the peatlands of Lough Barra bog, Meenachullion and Crockastoller.

The Park contains the two highest peaks in Donegal, Errigal (752m) and Slieve Snaght (683m). The steep-sided valley of Glenveagh holds the 5.5km-long Lough Veagh.

To the south of the Glendowan mountains lies the most extensive, intact lowland blanket bog in north-west Ireland. Parts of this peatland and the encircling hills are in the National Park. These areas are valued both for bogland vegetation and as habitat for certain bird species.

The full extent of the National Park is shown on the map inside the back cover.

A fine Victorian castle surrounded by beautiful gardens is picturesquely located on the eastern shore of the lake and provides the focal point for visitors to the Park.

Much of the land which comprise modern Glenveagh National Park was originally consolidated into a single holding in the 19th century by John George Adair, a wealthy land speculator from County Laois. The holding was managed as a private deer forest until 1975, when it was sold to the State and placed in the care of the Commissioners of Public Works to become a National Park. The last private owner of the estate, Henry P. McIlhenny, donated the castle, including much of its contents, and its gardens to the State upon his final departure from Glenveagh in 1983. The Park, and gardens were officially opened to the public in 1984 and the Castle in 1986.

The Park is the haunt of many rare and interesting plants and animals and is famous for its fine herd of red deer. The Park's natural features and landscapes are conserved, and facilities are provided for their appreciation and enjoyment by visitors, in accordance with the internationally accepted standards for managing national parks, as laid down by the World Conservation Union (IUCN).

Glenveagh National Park is managed by the National Parks and Wildlife Service which is now part of the Department of Arts, Culture and the Gaeltacht. It has become a major visitor attraction in the region providing visitor services, including a restaurant, mini-bus service and guided tours from Easter weekend until early November. Visitors may come to the Park during the rest of the year although visitor facilities are then closed.

The History of Glenveagh

Glenveagh is rarely alluded to in historical records, which is not really surprising when one considers how wild and remote it is, surrounded on all sides by expanses of trackless bog. This leaves us guessing as to its history from the time Ireland's first settlers reached our shores about 9,000 years ago until the area was permanently settled in the early 17th century. However, a little light has been thrown on this long period by records from nearby and related sites.

The archaeological record reveals that County Donegal was inhabited by an early wave of settlers, as flint instruments found in a number of places in the county are the work of Stone Age communities. These lived a nomadic life, hunting and fishing in one spot before moving on to another. They almost certainly visited Glenveagh, since it was then covered in forests in which deer and game were plentiful.

A later group of settlers were the Neolithic farmers who built great megalithic tombs in honour of their dead. The remains of many such tombs can be seen just twelve kilometres away on the Donegal coast between Falcarragh and Dunfanaghy. However, their builders left no visible traces in Glenveagh.

Neolithic communities were responsible for the widespread removal of tree cover from the uplands in most parts of Ireland as early as 5,000 years ago. The prevention of woodland regeneration by domestic animals, coupled with an already bad natural drainage, led to the retention of water on the surface and ultimately to the growth of peat bogs.

In Glenveagh, peat began to spread across the hills some 4,500 years ago and gradually replaced the pine forests that covered the mountain slopes. As the peat developed, it submerged all traces of human occupation. Glenveagh thereafter had poor soils and meagre woodlands and was of negligible value for farming. However, it must have continued to attract hunters and its remaining woodlands were undoubtedly exploited for their timber. It is also likely that local communities grazed their cattle and pigs on the mountain pastures each summer, and set up temporary dwellings on the hills for shelter and to protect their livestock from wolves, which survived in Ireland until the 18th century.

St. Columba, first Abbot of Iona

The only Early Christian settlements in the vicinity of Glenveagh were a short distance away to the east around Lough Gartan, where there is good arable land. One of Ireland's most famous missionaries, St. Columcille, also known as St. Columba, was born there in the year 521 AD.

His missionary work was in Scotland, where he founded the monastery of Iona.

The settlements at Gartan persisted through medieval times, with the people of Gartan and the Glenveagh hinterland following a relatively unchanging pastoral lifestyle, for the most part in peaceful isolation. Glenveagh itself remained virtually uninhabited until the plantation years of the 17th century. Settlement was to peak when an expanding population created a new and increasingly desperate demand for land in the 18th and early 19th centuries.

Years of Revolt (1595 - 1608)

In the 16th century, an English government in Dublin was actively seeking to impose its authority on this part of its dominion. Part of its strategy was to exploit family rivalries as, at that time, feuding Irish chieftains were not averse to enlisting English assistance for personal gain.

It was during this turbulent period, lasting into the early 17th century, that the valley of Glenveagh became refuge for a time to an army led by Cahir O'Doherty. Cahir's father, John O'Doherty, was chieftain of one of the most powerful families in north Donegal. In return for a knighthood, John O'Doherty agreed to surrender his lands to the reigning British monarch, Queen Elizabeth I. The lands were then re-granted to him under English rules of inheritance; thus he ensured that his lands and title would pass directly to his son and not be contested among the family, as was the Irish custom.

However, in 1595, a rebellion broke out against English rule and continued until 1601, when it was quelled by the decisive Battle of Kinsale in County Cork. During the rebellion, young Cahir O'Doherty was taken hostage by a leading local family, the O'Donnells, who wanted his father to fight against the English. Sir John O'Doherty was killed in the fighting and Cahir inherited his father's title and lands.

Doe Castle

Cahir's peace was short-lived, however, as the governor of Derry, a Royal appointee, quarrelled with him and caused him to believe he was to be cheated of his inheritance. In April 1608, Cahir O'Doherty marched on the city of Derry and set much of it on fire. Quickly moving west to Creeslough, near Glenveagh, he captured another stronghold of the north-west, Doe Castle.

Crown forces were soon on their way to Donegal to quell the revolt, and O'Doherty withdrew with his men to Glenveagh, from where he could launch attacks on his pursuers. Mullangore Wood in Glenveagh, where he hid, could only be approached from either end of the glen or through Glenlack, three easily defended routes.

Receiving news of the approach of a large English force, O'Doherty left Glenveagh in June 1608, and went quickly to Kincard, near Armagh, which he sacked. In July, he was returning to Doe Castle in Creeslough, which by now was under siege, when he was attacked and shot dead in Kilmacrenan. In the barbaric tradition of the time, his head was sent to adorn the spikes on the gates of Dublin Castle. His followers soon lost their will to fight and the last pockets of resistance were quickly subdued. In one of the final acts of suppression, Chichester, the Lord Deputy of Ireland, attacked and destroyed an 'island' fort on Lough Gartan. Though still a matter of conjecture, the evidence suggests that the fort was actually on the site of the present-day Glebe House, beside Lough Gartan.

Plantation and Settlement (1609 - 1800)
Following the suppression of the O'Dohertys, the British moved swiftly to install loyal supporters in Ulster, and the process of plantation began. To ensure that planters provided security for the Crown, the administration attached conditions to its land awards to grantees, and all had to undertake to plant their land with settlers.

Grantees usually disposed of their lands to one or more tenants through a 'grant in fee farm', which was a sort of perpetual leasehold. In return, they received a 'chief rent' every year. The tenant often re-let the lands and he, not the land-owner, was known as the landlord. The smaller tenants often let the lands in even smaller parcels, so the lowest rank of farming people occupied very small holdings and usually lived in extreme poverty.

In 1610, the lands of Glenveagh, including Derryveagh and Glendowan, were granted to eleven Irish citizens, one of whom was Lughaidh Ó Cléirigh, brother of Mícheál Ó Cléirigh, a co-author of the Annals of the Four Masters. By 1630, the whole area had been acquired by Sir Ralph Gore, son of a grantee who had been awarded lands near Manorhamilton, Co. Leitrim. A grandson of his became Chancellor of the Irish Exchequer. The north-eastern parts of Glenveagh were never granted because in 1608 they were held by the Church of Ireland.

The tenant farmers opened a route through the glen which today corresponds to the road from the Visitor Centre to Glenveagh Castle and the Upper Glen. The route was densely wooded, strewn with boulders and treacherously boggy in places, but it provided the shortest and most natural route through the Glenveagh mountains, from the Gweebarra valley in the south to Glenveagh Bridge in the north.

Traffic also moved between Gweebarra and the townland of Dunlewy, just west of Glenveagh. This followed a rugged and dangerous path across Crockballaghgeeha Gap and the precipitous slopes of the Poisoned Glen. It is the shortest and most logical route across the spine of the Derryveagh range but its former use as a traffic artery almost defies belief today.

Following the plantations, many of the dispossessed took to the hills and forests from where they raided and harassed the planters. They were known as 'tories', from the Irish word *tóraí*, meaning hunter. It is likely that some lived in Glenveagh.

Rory Oge O'More, a famous tory. (Illustration from 'The Image of Ireland')

Donegal's remaining woodlands were largely destroyed during this period. Many were clear-felled for cultivation by a rapidly growing population, and the demand for firewood and building timber put added pressure on the rest. Large quantities of timber were also consumed by charcoal-burning ironworks in places like Letterkenny and Milford. However, the woods surrounding Lough Veagh survived after many others disappeared and are believed to have been the last refuge of the native red deer in the county.

The Black Years (1800 - 1861)

The early 19th century was a bleak time for the Irish people and the majority lived in appalling conditions which we can scarcely imagine today. The peasantry was overcrowded, half-starved and often oppressed by landlords or their agents. The blackest depths of misery were reached following 1845 when the potato crop failed in successive years and the Great Famine ensued. More than a million people in Ireland starved to death or died of disease and a million more emigrated. A futile drainage scheme on the boggy slopes of Glenveagh offered relief work to starving labourers during this period. Traces of the narrow drains they dug can still be seen, though these are now largely overgrown.

The Famine Memorial, Letterkenny

An unmarked graveyard filled with dozens of famine victims was uncovered near the site of a former workhouse in Letterkenny in 1991 and testified to the impact of the Famine in County Donegal. A memorial near the County Museum now marks the spot.

Following the Famine, the tenant farmers remained at the mercy of their landlord because any improvements they made to their land became his property when the lease expired. Secondly, tenants had no security of tenure and could be evicted at will. Their troubles were compounded by the introduction of black-faced mountain sheep from Scotland in the 1850's. Buoyed by the prospect of making considerable profits from hitherto unyielding mountains, a number of Donegal landlords annexed upland areas which had formerly been commonage and stocked them with sheep. Tenant farmers suddenly found they were being denied the right to take their livestock to the hills for the summer months, as they had been doing for generations. In Glenveagh, they fell foul of the ruthless landlord, John George Adair.

Ramelton
Burt Castle
Aran Island
TIR CHONAILL
GLENVEAGH NATIONAL PARK
Derry
12

John George Adair

John George Adair, born in 1823, was the only son of George Adair of the Bellegrove estate near Ballybrittas, County Laois (then known as the Queen's County). He came into the holdings of a minor landed family and transformed his fortune during a career of adventurous land speculation and mortgaging. He also bought land in the Encumbered Estates Court which was established after the Famine to recover debts from bankrupt landlords. Perhaps surprisingly, he was involved in the Young Ireland movement and stood as a Tenants' Rights candidate for the constituency of Limerick in 1852.

Adair first saw Glenveagh in 1857 while on a tour of the area and, in his own words, he was *'enchanted by the surpassing beauty of the scenery'.* After his visit, he immediately began planning to buy the property. His plans included building a castle for himself on the estate. This was designed by John Townsend Trench, a cousin of Adair's.

Sketch of Glenveagh Castle by Townend Trench

He purchased the chief rent of Derryveagh and Glendowan in 1857 and bought out the interests of the major tenants. He also bought from the ecclesiastical commissioners the lands from Gartan to Devlin. By 1859, the estate totalled 11,300 hectares.

The lands at the lower end of Lough Veagh around 1900, showing the Police Barracks

Once in possession of Glenveagh, Adair thought it wise to erect a police barracks for the Royal Irish Constabulary. The barracks, located at Glenveagh Bridge near the Visitor Centre, was enlarged twice during the 20th century and is now a private residence. It merited a mention in *Rotha Mór an tSaoil*, the autobiography of Mícheál MacGabhann, who was from Cloghaneely on the west coast of Donegal. As a youngster in the summer of 1874, Mícheál was sent to herd cattle on Meenadreen in Glenveagh. He befriended one of the RIC officers in the barracks, John McDonnell from County Armagh, and became a frequent visitor.

Adair also built a pound for 'trespassing' livestock, even though there were no fences to stop livestock from straying, as tenants could rarely afford such a luxury. Besides collecting fines for straying animals and prosecuting a number of tenants for alleged sheep-stealing, Adair caused further ill-feeling by bringing Scotsmen to work on his estate. Some of these were of dubious character and one, James Murray, was implicated in the disappearance of 85 sheep. Murray was hated locally for extracting fines for the return of strays, and one November day in 1860, while rounding up sheep on Farscollop mountain, he was murdered.

John Adair felt that the tenants were conspiring against him and he resolved to make them pay dearly. At the beginning of 1860 he had served notice on his tenants to quit in order to resolve some farm boundary disputes. Once these were resolved, the tenants should quickly have regained possession. However, Adair decided to be rid of the lot of them. There was no evidence whatsoever of a conspiracy against him, and neighbouring landlords vouched for the integrity of the tenantry, but in the face of mounting disquiet at government level, Adair set about evicting them all.

Remains of an Eviction Cottage at Derryveagh

The majority of Adair's tenants lived beside Lough Gartan in the most fertile part of the estate. Others lived in Glendowan and at the head of the Gweebarra valley. Few families lived in the glen itself, though some estate workers, and almost certainly Adair himself, lived near the southern end in stone cottages whose remains can still be seen today. Derrylahan, by the northern end of Lough Veagh, held four families.

The evictions of 46 families, involving 244 people, were carried out in April 1861. Some 200 militia men were sent to keep the peace while the sheriff ejected the tenants. The first to be evicted was a widow named McAward, aged 60, who lived by Lough Barra with six daughters and a son. When their house was levelled by the sheriff and his men, they became frantic with despair. Harrowing scenes accompanied all of the evictions, which took three full days to complete, and in nearly every house there was someone of advanced years for whom eviction meant certain death.

Some of the evicted found homes with relatives, and others went to the workhouse in Letterkenny. Nearly 150, however, emigrated to Australia where for many years their fate remained a mystery. But in 1982, an Australian historian, Dr. Bernard Barrett, traced their arrival and subsequent progress in Sydney. They did well there and some of their descendants still live near Sydney.

Cornelia Adair

Glenveagh since 1861

In the middle of the 1860's, with plans in train for Glenveagh Castle, Adair began to look to new business opportunities in America, where he managed to increase his fortune still further through brokerage and ranching. While in the United States, he met a wealthy young widow called Cornelia Ritchie (née Wadsworth, from Geneseo, New York) whose husband had died in the American Civil War. They married in 1869, when Adair was forty-six years of age and she thirty-one. Adair brought his wife home to Bellegrove, where he remodelled his house for her. He then began work on Glenveagh Castle, which he completed in 1873. The castle's first guests were invited that year, but the flow of visitors was to remain quite small until Cornelia Adair introduced deer-stalking in the 1890's.

The couple began to spend increasing amounts of time in America, where they developed new business interests and travelled extensively. In 1875, Adair moved his brokerage to Denver, Colorado, and the following year founded his most successful business, the J.A. Ranch, in the Palo Duro Canyon, Texas. On his way home from a third visit to the ranch in 1885, Adair died suddenly in St. Louis, Missouri. His wife thereafter paid an annual autumn visit to the ranch, which continued to prosper. It held 100,000 cattle in 1889, and by 1903 was 405,000 hectares in size with a further 810,000 hectares leased.

In 1887, the house at Bellegrove burned down, compelling Mrs. Adair to move into a smaller house on the Bellegrove estate. The fire had a positive outcome for Glenveagh, however, as it resulted in her entertaining more at the castle. Over the next 30 years, she opted to spend most of her time in Glenveagh where she became a society hostess of note, and became well-liked in the locality. She continually sought to improve the castle's comforts and the beauty of its grounds, carrying out major improvements to the estate and laying out the gardens.

GLENVEAGH
NATIONAL
PARK

Aran
Island

Burt Castle

Der

16

View from Mrs. Adair's seat

She also created a sylvan walk through the heart of Mullangore Wood ascending to a view point. The pathway and steps running up into the wood and following Glenlack stream may still be seen today, as may the many exotic species she planted there, including European larch, pine, spruce, beech, fir and sycamore. Less enlightened was the introduction of *Rhododendron ponticum* to Glenveagh Gardens and the Upper Glen sometime around 1900. This hardy exotic shrub quickly spread to the surrounding woodlands and hillsides.

In order to develop a deer herd for deer-stalking at Glenveagh, Mrs. Adair purchased red deer from stocks in Britain and from elsewhere in Ireland and she received a gift of a stag from King Edward VII. Also in 1891, she ordered a deer fence for the estate to facilitate herd management. The 1.8m-tall fence, runs for 45km across mountain and bog.

Mrs Adair's house party August 1901. Standing centre is Lord Kitchener, the World War I British Field Marshal

The following decade saw a stream of visitors coming to Glenveagh for the deer-stalking, and the pinnacle of Mrs. Adair's entertaining was undoubtedly reached in 1902 when her house parties included the Duke and Duchess of Connaught and Lord Kitchener. The latter is famous for a World War I poster in which he exhorts young men to enlist with the words 'Your Country Needs You'.

The outbreak of the First World War in 1914 sounded the death-knell for Edwardian country-house living, both here and in Britain. Mrs. Adair, who had become a British subject, put Glenveagh to use in the war effort by housing some 30 Belgian war wounded who are remembered for a path they constructed in the gardens. She continued to summer at the castle until 1916, but thereafter stayed in England, where she died in 1921 at the age of eighty-three.

In early 1922, during the Civil War that followed Irish Independence, the castle was occupied by the 'Irregulars', or anti-Treaty forces, who stationed outposts in the gate lodges and used the remote valley as a centre of operations. In July 1922, soldiers of the Free State Army moved on the castle and forced the Irregulars to withdraw. The new occupants remained until 1925.

As the Adairs' marriage had no issue, the estate had been inherited on Mrs. Adair's death by her grandson by her first marriage but, by 1925, it was a much sadder enterprise than the one she had left. The deer fence, for example, had been looted for its wire, allowing much of the herd to escape. However, the estate found a tenant in Captain Geoffrey Gathorne-Hardy, an English veteran of the Boer and First World Wars, who took it for the hunting. He rented Glenveagh from 1925 until 1928.

The castle remained on the market until 1929, when it was sold to a scholar, a Harvard professor of fine arts with a special interest in medieval art and architecture, thus maintaining the American link. The new owner, Arthur Kingsley Porter, had already spent much of his life in Europe, tracing the development of Romanesque architecture and sculpture in Italy, France and Spain. He came to Ireland to study Irish archaeology and culture. He and his

Arthur Kingsley Porter

wife Lucy had the castle repaired and also rebuilt the deer fence. The Kingsley Porters mainly entertained Irish literary and artistic figures, and one small vestige of their residency is the collection of paintings by Æ (George Russell), whose interest in the Celtic revival and Irish mythology may have been of some help to his host. Kingsley Porter's research soon resulted in a volume published in 1931 entitled 'The Crosses and Culture of Ireland' which he had not expected to be his last.

Kingsley Porter had built himself a hermit's hut on Inishbofin, an island off the Donegal coast. While staying on the island with his wife in July 1933, he went out for a walk by the shore one day and never returned. He is presumed to have drowned.

Inishbofin Island, Co. Donegal

Understandably, Donegal held less attraction for Mrs. Kingsley Porter thereafter and in 1934 she leased the estate for the summer to other Americans - a Mrs. McIlhenny of Philadelphia and her son, Henry Plumer McIlhenny. Following a return visit in 1936, Henry McIlhenny took up an option that had stood from their first visit and bought the estate.

John McIlhenny born 1830

Henry McIlhenny was an Irish-American whose grandfather, John McIlhenny, was born in 1830 in Carrigart, a few miles north of Glenveagh. John McIlhenny grew up in Milford, where his father had had a shop. John emigrated to Columbus, Georgia, where he was elected city mayor, a post he held for 20 years. He finally settled in Philadelphia, where he amassed a considerable fortune, largely through his invention of the first gas meter. His son, John, was also a very successful industrialist, but in later life became deeply involved in collecting works of art and antiques. For the seven years before his death in 1925, he was president of the Philadelphia Museum of Art. His son, Henry, inherited his artistic instinct and art collecting became the focus of his own life.

Henry McIlhenny

Henry McIlhenny entered Harvard University to study fine art in 1929 and at the same time began his first art collection, concentrating on 19th century French Impressionist painting. In 1934, he joined the staff of the Philadelphia Museum of Art, where his duties allowed him long summer absences which greatly facilitated his annual visits to Glenveagh.

On buying the Castle, he at once started to search for contents to go with the building, but his plans were interrupted by the outbreak of the Second World War in 1939. He served with the American Navy for the period of the war, but by 1947, was able to return to Glenveagh and to its redecoration.

From then until 1983, he stayed for several months each year at Glenveagh, where he devoted much time to restoring the castle and developing its gardens. He was visited at his remote hide-away by leading figures of international society, including the screen actors Greta Garbo and Grace Kelly, and he carried on the 'Big House' lifestyle until his departure, though it had died out in almost all Irish country houses many years before. After Henry McIlhenny retired from the museum in 1964 - immediately becoming a trustee and later chairman of the board - he had more time to enjoy Glenveagh, and his summer visits often extended to five months. Under his watchful stewardship, and with the assistance of his estate manager, Julian Burkitt, Glenveagh blossomed. Plants were sent to his gardens from all over the world and new areas of the gardens were planted and developed. A swimming pool was built by the lakeside. But Henry McIlhenny was not about to become a recluse among his plants. Chauffeurs went weekly to Shannon and Belfast to collect and despatch visitors, while many more came under their own steam. The Castle was filled with busy staff. Each evening, sumptuous meals were prepared by the Castle housekeeper, Nellie Gallagher from Dunlewy, and were served in the Castle dining room by her brother Patrick, the butler. Guests were often treated to picnics at the Stalking Hut, close to the 200 metre high waterfall beyond the lake. This period in Glenveagh's history was remembered by Mr. McIlhenny's guests as a golden age.

Mr McIlhenny with head gardener Matt Armour (left)

Eventually, Henry McIlhenny began to find the travelling to and from Ireland too demanding, and the upkeep of the estate was also becoming a strain. In 1975, he agreed the sale of the Glenveagh Estate to the Office of Public Works, allowing for the creation of a National Park. In 1983, he bestowed the castle on the Nation, along with the gardens. He died unexpectedly in Philadelphia in 1986, at the age of 75. Glenveagh National Park opened to the public in 1984, while the Castle was opened in 1986, a few months after its last private owner had passed away.

Glenveagh Castle

Glenveagh Castle is a 19th century castellated mansion and was built between 1867 and 1873. Its construction in a remote mountain setting was inspired by the Victorian idyll of a romantic highland retreat. It was designed by John Townsend Trench, a cousin of its builder and first owner, John George Adair, with whom he had been raised in County Laois. Although not a professional architect, Trench had a hand in at least one other building: he designed the Gothic town hall in Arklow, built in 1878.

Glenveagh Castle from the air, looking southwest along the glen

Ramelton
Burt Castle
GLENVEAGH
NATIONAL
PARK
Aran
Island
Derr

The castle style remained a dominant idiom in country house building throughout the 19th century, but by the 1860's, when work began at Glenveagh, it was fast becoming unfashionable although a last great boost to the castle style was Queen Victoria's rebuilding of Balmoral in 1853-55 in a Scottish Baronial manner, to designs partly by Prince Albert. The 1860's also saw a number of other castles built in remote scenic areas in Ireland, most notably Kylemore Castle (now Abbey), which was built by the Manchester financier Mitchell Henry, and Ashford Castle, completed for Sir Arthur Guinness in 1870.

Twenty years after the completion of Glenveagh Castle, a new castle would have been a rarity among the Renaissance palazzi and Queen Anne houses then fashionable among the newly rich. But Adair already had an up-to-date country house at Bellegrove in County Laois. A mountain retreat was its ideal complement and a hunting estate had permanent appeal.

Glenveagh Castle under construction circa 1871

Glenveagh Castle was sited on a small promontory jutting into Lough Veagh, with fine views along the glen. It was designed to resemble Balmoral on a reduced scale, and duly included a four-storey rectangular keep with turrets.

The designer also appears to have imitated the style of earlier Irish tower-houses, which over the years had acquired lower, less defensive and more modern extensions and he added two wings, which surround the courtyard at the main entrance. These imparted an air of antiquity to the property.

The building stone chosen was granite, plentiful in Donegal but difficult to work and allowing for little detail. The final effect depended largely on the bold keep tower with its distinctively stepped battlements. The latter, having been discovered by antiquarians of the period to be peculiar to Ireland, became an almost inescapable touch. The silhouette of the keep is enlivened by a few roughly medieval details, including corner turrets or bartizans with decorative arrow-loops, and a crowning mock watch-tower. However, the castle's greatest distinction remains its setting.

The private ownership of Glenveagh Castle has always involved an American connection, from Cornelia Adair, wife of its builder and first owner, to the Philadelphian collector, Henry Plumer McIlhenny, who made a gift of it to the Nation.

Following the death of John George Adair in 1885, Cornelia decided to extend the Castle, and she turned what had begun as a comfortable hunting lodge into a spacious building with a country house atmosphere. A new wing containing the present hall and a big billiard room (now the drawing room) was opened in 1888 and a round tower was added to its gable in 1901.

After Mrs. Adair's death in 1921, the condition of the castle declined considerably and her grandson, who inherited the property, was not inclined to embark on restoration. Most of the castle's panelling was burnt as firewood and little furniture was left in place. When the castle was bought in 1929 by Arthur Kingsley Porter of Harvard University, he and his wife Lucy had it repaired and redecorated in a modest fashion. A conical roof was added to the round tower, and inside, the rooms were painted, the hall was patterned with shells, and some of Mrs. Adair's furniture, bought back at auction, was reinstalled.

Henry McIlhenny bought the estate in 1937 and the present appearance of the castle is the result of his continual refinements to it. He strove to soften the castle's outwardly hard and inelegant style by developing lush gardens around it and by adding variety and luxury to its interior. He initially sought out 18th century Irish furniture and silver and planned to have pictures from the same period. By the late 1940's, however, he had begun to buy the Victorian paintings, many by Edwin Landseer, which would form the nucleus of his second art collection.

'Night' by Edwin Landseer

No artist of the period could have suited Glenveagh more than Landseer, an English artist renowned for his paintings of deer, and Henry McIlhenny made a pursuit of acquiring his pictures. In 1956, he bought two of Landseer's greatest works, 'Night' and 'Morning', and eventually owned 15 of his paintings, which formed a perfect focus for the deer theme that Mr. McIlhenny made a central feature of Glenveagh.

The forbidding architecture of the castle is quickly forgotten amidst the varied comforts within. Although primarily interested in painting, Mr. McIlhenny served the Philadelphia Museum of Art as Curator of Decorative Arts and his expertise in this field is evident throughout the castle. Through time, each room acquired a different character relating to its function, some roughly in keeping with the period of the house, others freely inventive. Though most items were obtained overseas, some furniture, including the Georgian marble fireplaces, were brought from Ards House near Creeslough, a few miles north of Glenveagh, prior to its demolition in 1966.

Following Henry McIlhenny's donation of Glenveagh Castle to the Nation in 1983, it underwent some essential repairs before being opened to the public in 1986. Apart from the most important paintings, furniture and silver, which Mr. McIlhenny left to the museum in Philadelphia, the contents of the castle remain in place. The colour schemes and arrangements have also been retained. The furniture is a lovely mix of George III, Regency and Victorian, with some pieces from other periods and a number of more unusual items from around the world. The Landseer paintings have been replaced by contemporary engravings and prints of the artist's work.

Few of the great houses of Ireland are preserved in this condition, with their original furnishings, and in Glenveagh Castle one catches a glimpse of a lifestyle belonging to an earlier age. The National Parks and Wildlife Service maintains the castle as the centre-piece of Glenveagh National Park, and the castle welcomes visitors during the same months as all of its former owners did - from mid-spring to early autumn.

Aran
Island

GLENVEAGH
NATIONAL
PARK

Burt Castle

Derr

26

The Castle's Interior

Each room in the castle has its own style, colour and décor, designed by Mr. McIlhenny to complement their individual functions. A room-by-room account is presented below.

The Hall

The entrance to Glenveagh Castle is very attractive but surprisingly modest. The front door opens into a unimposing barrel-vaulted room, more corridor than hall, with neither the scale nor ceremony one might expect in a castle. Like the narrow corridors throughout the building, the hall is basically functional and has the air of being added on, as indeed it was, when Mrs. Adair extended a new wing from the keep tower in 1888. Glenveagh was always a summer home to its owners and is expressed in the hall's shell decoration, which were designed by Kingsley Porter and crafted by Matt Armour and Jimmy Brady early in the 1930's.

Stags' heads introduce the deer theme prominent throughout the house. A pair made from marbleised plaster flank the door, while on the wall are a pair of 19th century carved heads with natural antlers, believed to be German. The blanket chest contained travelling rugs and towels for swimmers. Sitting on the chest is a painted wood figure of the Taoist god, Xianan.

The Drawing Room

After the shallow hall, the drawing room comes as a surprise. A spacious formal room, its soft colours and rich textures differ sharply from the stark black and white of the entrance. It is on the ground floor of the wing added by Mrs. Adair, and was built as a billiard room and is where most of the socialising took place.The room was redecorated after World War II by Henry McIlhenny who appointed mainly George III furniture, including sofas, chairs, stools and two mahogany bookcases, the larger one with Gothic glazing. The rugs were made in Killybegs to designs copied at Mr. McIlhenny's request from the English material of the seat covers. The 18th century white marble mantelpiece was brought from Ards. To one side of it is an 18th century pole screen used to shield the wax make-up of the ladies from the heat. It depicts a stag. To the other side is a celestial globe, dated 1876, which most likely had a terrestrial twin. The room also contains a pier glass, an Irish-made square piano, an inlaid table, busts of Homer and Mycaenas and a selection of paintings.

GLENVEAGH
NATIONAL
PARK

Ramelton

Burt Castle

Aran
Island

Derr

28

The Dining Room

Without its gleaming abundance of silver - and more so, the guests who gathered here four times each day - the dining room has something of a sparse air. But its decoration was always deliberately spare, depending on a few pieces to give it an appropriately sober elegance. Here, Mr. McIlhenny entertained his guests with warm hospitality and attention to detail. Dinner was always held by candlelight. He continually varied the tableware and, to augment it, commissioned from Salzburg the dinner and tea service laid out here. Its 365 pieces bear a prancing stag coloured in the pale Glenveagh green. The ochre marble of the mid 18th century fireplace sets a colour tone for the fabrics, including the printed cotton screen and the Donegal tweed of the seats and curtains. The screen masks an already concealed door cut into the wall and giving access to the pantry. At the other end of the room a false door on the right answers the entrance symmetrically. The giltwood mirror is of a period with the fireplace. The carpets are Portuguese.

The outstanding feature of this room was a pair of Landseer canvasses which Mr. McIlhenny left to the Philadelphia Museum of Art. A powerful climax to the deer theme at Glenveagh, 'Night' and 'Morning' represent a fatal battle between two great stags. The original paintings have been replaced with reproductions.

The Study

The study - or Red Room - best typifies the air of comfortable formality that pervades the castle. It is a luxurious room, with its deep mahogany and white enveloped by a stately crimson, Henry McIlhenny's favourite colour. It served as both a study and a sitting room. Golden retrievers padded around or slept on a couch by the turf fire, enjoying the peace. The fireplace, like several others, came from Ards. The mantelpiece has an inset panel painted to imitate a Byzantine mosaic tile. Above it is an 18th century walnut and gilt mirror. The room is enriched with gilt and brass, including a pair of mirrors carved as military trophies. An early 19th century Anglo-Indian table, with masks in place of drawer handles, was introduced by the Kingsley Porters.

Alleviating the richness are some plain white porcelain ornaments, including a pair of elephants supporting obelisks and two pen trays in the shape of tortoises, with their shells as lids. The room contained several Victorian paintings. Above the George III bureau is a reproduction of one, John Calcott Horsley's 'Lovers Under a Blossom Tree'.

GLENVEAGH
NATIONAL
PARK

Burt Castle

Aran
Island

30

The Music Room

The music room, on the ground floor of the round tower, no longer has its grand piano but contains an Irish harp dating from about 1840. Mr. McIlhenny made the room a light-hearted reminder of the parallels between Glenveagh and Balmoral. Its cloth wall-covering, the Gordon Clan tartan, would alert any who missed the connection, but was also intended to improve its acoustic properties. The mirror and the chandelier use antlers from various deer species, along with wild boar tusks. There are Victorian tables of antelope horn and brass, doorstops cast in the form of stags and fruitwood brackets carved as trophies of the hunt. When he left Glenveagh, Mr. McIlhenny donated the grand piano to the church in Ramelton where his great grand-parents were married.

The Music Room

The Library

The library, situated on the first floor of the keep and above the study, was mainly used as a daytime sitting room, offering fine views across the lake and along the valley. Mr. McIlhenny added to its decoration while retaining much of what was left there by Kingsley Porter, including the four paintings by Æ (George Russell). The Italian Garden, flanked by August-flowering *Eucryphia* trees, was designed to be viewed from this room. Eighteen century Irish tables stand in the window bays, their dark mahogany colour picking up the other dark furniture - a big bookcase, a lacquered Italian box and teabin lamps. In the corner, over a George III bureau, is a 15th century Italian carved saint.

The Library

The Master Bedroom

Like the study, this room is an essay in crimson and mahogany. Most of the furniture is Regency, including the mahogany four-poster bed which Mrs. Kingsley Porter brought to Glenveagh.

The Master Bedroom

In the corner to the left is a small architect's table with a hinged top. The armchairs and big wardrobe are Victorian. The painting 'A Stag and Doe in the Highlands' is by Byron Webb, a long-forgotten Victorian artist whose work, like others of the period, is receiving new attention. It is dated 1861, the year of the Derryveagh evictions.

The all white en suite bathroom was converted from a bedroom in the 1960s, when Mr. McIlhenny panelled the walls with shutters from Ards. Above the fireplace, also from Ards, hangs three steel engravings after statues in the Vatican by Canova - Apollo, Belvedere and Hercules. The chandeliers of Venetian glass are modern.

The Blue Room
In each storey of the round tower is an oval room within a circle, with corridors, cupboards or bathrooms fitted into the space left over. Here on the first floor, an alcove extending from the oval contains a bathroom and wardrobe. The cleverness of the arrangement is enhanced by the fire, whose flue runs around the window above it. However, the engineering never matched the idea and the fire always drew poorly, often filling the room with smoke.

The bedroom - furnished in an American style - is blue in colour, which is said to have been Mrs. Adair's choice. Its lightness in tone is mirrored in pale

oak and satinwood furniture, including a Victorian davenport, American beds and the sofa table in the alcove. Around the walls are gouache sketches of the Pantheon, the Trevi Fountain and other monuments in Rome, a city where, for a time, Henry McIlhenny worked at the American Academy.

The Pink Room

Forming the top floor of the round tower, the Pink Bedroom has an oriental air, with some of the furnishings being inlaid with mother-of-pearl in the Chinese style of which the Victorians were so fond. The room's mirrors are inlaid in this way and decorated with gilt Chinese designs. Most of the small pieces of lacquered or ebonised furniture are made of papier-maché and give an idea of the variety of items that were pressed from this material in the 19th century, including chairs, stools, games-tables, nests, dressing-tables, mirrors, clocks, lockers and cabinets. This method began as a cheaper version of the Chinese lacquered furniture that appeared in Europe in the 17th century.

The bedroom was originally partitioned and housed two maids. One of them would have enjoyed better views than some of the guests and so it duly became a guest room.

Glenveagh Gardens

Many famous Irish gardens are set in natural landscapes of great beauty and nowhere else is the contrast between the luxuriance of the Gardens and a rugged and exposed environment as marked as at Glenveagh. Situated at the foot of a steep, wooded hillside sloping down to Glenveagh Castle on the windswept shore of Lough Veagh, the uncompromising conditions of high rainfall and acid soil have been successfully exploited and the Gardens feature a range of exotic plants from places as far afield as South America, Tasmania and China. The acid soil is particularly suited to the growth of rhododendrons, of which there is a fine collection.

The Castle, Gardens, Boathouse and Swimming Pool

Much of the general layout of the Gardens dates from the ownership of Cornelia Adair. She planted shelter-belts of Scots pine and rhododendron and laid out the Pleasure Grounds - gardens were often called the 'Pleasure Grounds' in Victorian times to distinguish them from the kitchen garden, then often known simply as 'the garden'. Her work laid the basis for more recent plantings.

The transformation of Glenveagh into one of Ireland's foremost gardens, imaginatively designed and supporting a rich variety of rare and tender plants, was the work of Henry McIlhenny, who personally supervised its development from 1937 until 1983. The Gardens presented a daunting challenge, with *Rhododendron ponticum* and bamboo run wild, though some exceptional plants of earlier plantings remained. These included specimens of two large-leaved rhododendrons, *Rhododendron falconeri* and *R. arboreum*. The Belgian Walk, built by wounded Belgian soldiers during the First World War, had also survived. Mr. McIlhenny began collecting plants from all over the world, and his knowledge of plants and sense of artistry were augmented by expert landscaping advice, firstly from James Russell and then from Lanning Roper.

A renowned English nurseryman, James Russell came to work in Glenveagh in 1953. The late Lanning Roper was born in New Jersey and studied in Harvard with Henry McIlhenny before settling in England. Regarded as one of the outstanding garden designers of his time, he worked, amongst other Irish gardens, in Glenveagh, Trinity College Dublin, Castlecoole and Marble Hill. The plans of Russell and Roper were implemented by Glenveagh estate staff, particularly Matt Armour who came to Glenveagh in 1930 and served as head gardener throughout the McIlhenny years.

Rhododendron 'Polar Bear'

James Russell advised the expansion of Cornelia Adair's rhododendron collection. His two-themed approach was to plant large-leaved rhododendrons for their noble form and scented rhododendrons for their fragrance. The latter are often tender, but the milder microclimate of the Gardens has suited *Rhododendron* 'Polar Bear', *R. ciliatum, R. lindleyi* and others.

Russell also made creative use of a rocky gully carpeted with moss and fern under a canopy of oak, which descends the hillside behind the castle. He built a scenic stone path up the gully, and along one flank constructed a steep flight of 67 stone steps leading to a high, grassy belvedere which overlooks the Castle and the Gardens in their lakeside setting. Lanning Roper helped Henry McIlhenny design an Italianate terrace on the Belgian Walk. The stone-flagged, walled terrace uses stone and marble sculpture from Florence. It adds formality to the natural features of the walk.

Mr. McIlhenny replanted the Belgian Walk, the Twelve Step Path and the View Garden. Along the lakeshore to the south of the castle, he created the Swiss Walk and a formal Italian Garden. He enhanced the exotic nature of the Pleasure Grounds by adding to its tree ferns, palms and rhododendrons and he provided ground cover with beds of *Gunnera*, hostas and lilies; the latter being one of his specialties.

The Walled Garden

In later years, Mr. McIlhenny turned a kitchen garden behind the Castle into a walled garden, planted in an antiquated style. It gives the impression of being centuries old, but in fact was built in 1957. At the top of the Walled Garden and adjoining the Castle he built a neo-Gothic conservatory to designs by Philippe Jullian, a French cultural historian.

Mr. McIlhenny planted the Gardens for effect rather than to show off individual plants. He gave each section of the Gardens its own character and style and linked them all together with winding paths. With clever planning, the Gardens feature a range of plants that create interest and colour throughout the year. However, he was particularly pleased with his late-flowering plants, including several fine specimens of *Hoheria* and *Eucryphia*. At all times of the year, the rugged grandeur of the setting contrasts vividly with the studied luxuriance of the plantings, and this remains the gardens' greatest distinction.

In 1983, the Office of Public Works assumed responsibility for the Gardens and they were opened to the public in 1984. A tour with 18 numbered stops is marked through the Gardens, closely following the route that Henry McIlhenny favoured when showing his guests around. You should allow at least one hour for the full tour, but if you have insufficient time to complete it, you can return quickly to the start from most points.

The Orangerie and Walled Garden

Plan of Gardens

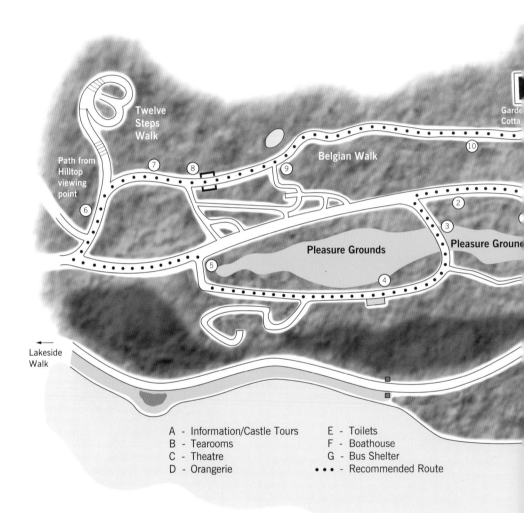

Twelve Steps Walk

Belgian Walk

Garde Cotta

Path from Hilltop viewing point

Pleasure Grounds

Pleasure Groun

Lakeside Walk

A - Information/Castle Tours
B - Tearooms
C - Theatre
D - Orangerie

E - Toilets
F - Boathouse
G - Bus Shelter
••• - Recommended Route

GLENVEAGH NATIONAL PARK

Kamelton

Burt Castle

Derr

Aran Island

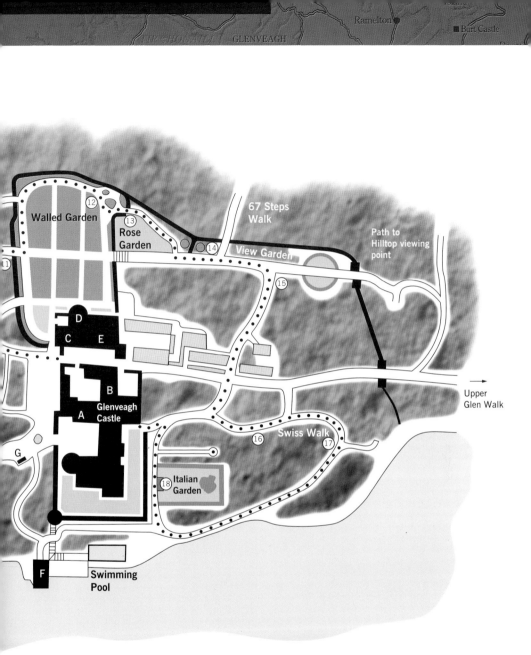

Ramelton ■ Burt Castle

GLENVEAGH

Walled Garden

⑫

⑬ Rose Garden

67 Steps Walk

⑭ View Garden

Path to Hilltop viewing point

⑮

D

C E

B

A Glenveagh Castle

⑯ Swiss Walk ⑰

Upper Glen Walk

G

⑱ Italian Garden

F Swimming Pool

GLENVEAGH
NATIONAL
PARK

Aran
Island

Burt Castle

Derr

The Garden Tour

Stop 1 The tour begins at the entrance to the Pleasure Grounds, where a fine *Rhododendron arboreum* grows on the upper side of the path. The eye is drawn to the striking foliage of the Australasian tree ferns *Dicksonia antarctica* and the Chusan palms *Trachycarpus fortunei* from China.

Stop 2 The fine Katsura tree *Cercidiphyllum japonicum* by the path has both a beautiful shape and wonderful autumn colour. Nearby you can see fine specimens of the tree rhododendrons *Rhododendron falconeri* and *R. sino-grande,* which were transplanted from Mulroy House near Carrigart around 1950. They have very large leaves and pale yellow blossoms.

The Pleasure Grounds in early June

Stop 3 The centre-piece of the Pleasure Grounds is a long irregular lawn fringed by herbaceous plants and backed by trees and shrubs. The lawn fulfils a similar role to a garden lake or pond, providing a smooth, restful surface that is easy on the eye.

On your right are bright Japanese azaleas, and on your left a tall Atlantic blue cedar *Cedrus atlantica* 'Glauca' with a Chusan palm and tree ferns below it. Notice the layered foliage and bright green leaves of the outstanding *Trochodendron aralioides* trees beside the shelter-belt of tall pines to your left. *Gunnera manicata,* resembling giant rhubarb, can be seen on the lawn.

Stop 4 Statues, urns and other sculptural works are a feature of Glenveagh Gardens. Some are part of formal elements, while others are used in less formal settings such as here in the Pleasure Grounds. Many items are Italian, but the statues here are from Bali in Indonesia.

Behind the stone seat, there is a bank of the tiny-leaved rhododendron, *R. cinnabarinum,* and a slope that is silvery with *Senecio,* a genus which is related to the common ragwort. The senecios include the well-known *Senecio* Dunedin Hybrid and the more unusual *S. elaeagnifolius* and *S. hectoris.* From the vantage point of the stone seat, you can admire a selection of tall southern beeches on the far side of the lawn. Two are evergreen - *Nothofagus dombeyi* and *N. procera* - while *N. obliqua* (coated in lichen) is deciduous. Two kinds of magnolia flourish by the southern beeches - *Magnolia tripetala,* or umbrella tree, and *M. salicifolia.*

Japanese Maple

By the edge of the path, notice the remarkable, spindly *Pseudopanax* species, which are rare, and the *Rhododendron* 'Kwayii Cross', whose pink blooms and the Arum lilies on the ground below create a colourful spectacle. Lilies are a recurring theme in the Gardens and the atmosphere is laden with their heavy fragrance in summer.

Further along the path is one of several fine Japanese maples *Acer palmatum* 'Atropurpureum'. The red leaves of the maple provide colour long after the flowers of the rhododendrons have fallen. Notice also the small red-barked tree, *Stuartia koreana,* whose fragrant white flowers give way to the rich autumn colours of the leaves.

Stop 5 From this vantage point you can see how the Pleasure Grounds echo the lake below, with a long expanse of lawn surrounded by waves of herbaceous beds. The trees and bushes mimic the steep slopes above.

The great, red-barked conifer at the corner is an old specimen of *Cryptomeria japonica* 'Elegans'. The herbaceous border of *Hosta* is one of several in the garden. At the next turn, there is a delightful snowdrop tree *Styrax japonica,* which has masses of pendulous white flowers in June.

Griselinia Tree

Leaving the Pleasure Grounds, you pass between gate piers adorned with statues of deer. On your right is a rare Chilean hazel *Gevuina avellana,* which resembles holly. Further on, the tender species *Michelia doltsopa* has attained a considerable height; it is a relative of the magnolia. A large, old *Griselinia* dating from Cornelia Adair's time is situated at the corner where the path turns right.

Stop 6 After passing the end of The Viewpoint Trail (see p.121), you reach a view of a 4m-high pillar with a stone pineapple which harks back to a time when pineapples were a luxury only the rich could afford. Notice the spear-like New Zealand flax *Phormium tenax* in the foreground.

A few metres further on to your left, a narrow path leads up to a rocky knoll. This short optional climb is known as the Twelve Step Path and features specimens of several tender plants, including the pink-leaved *Pseudowintera colorata, Rhododendron megacalyx, R. johnstoneanum* (double- and single-flowered forms) and the fragrant *R. lindleyi.* Retrace your steps to get back on the route.

Stop 7 You are now on the Belgian Walk. On the right is a tall clump of *Eucryphia moorei,* a Tasmanian evergreen which is rarely seen in Irish gardens. The path is fringed with Japanese azaleas.

Stop 8 The Italianate Terrace, built in 1966, is one of the newest features in the Gardens. It is floored with Donegal slate and furnished with antique stone statuary, mainly 18th century Italian. There are also many large earthenware pots planted with azaleas and hostas.

At the entrance to the terrace, is a slender Italian cypress *Cupressus sempervirens* and an excellent *Metrosideros lucida,* a tender evergreen bush which produces striking red flowers in summer. The beds behind the wall on the left are cultivated with *Rhododendron ciliatum,* which displays a profusion of pale pink flowers in spring. Sturdy examples of *Pieris* 'Forest Flame' and

The Italianate Terrace

P. formosa 'Wakehurst' grow at the exit. The scarlet young foliage of the *Pieris formosa* is accentuated by the grey stonework. Pink and red colours suffuse the terrace in due season.

As you leave the terrace, look down to your right to see a tall plant like a date palm among some exotic pines. This is *Cordyline indivisa,* a tender relative of the common *C. australis,* which can also be seen in the Gardens. On your left you can see the crimson-flowered *Rhododendron* 'Mulroy Vanguard', which was registered with the Royal Horticultural Society in 1985.

Stop 9 To your right, you pass a group of South American trees, including a Chilean conifer, *Podocarpus salignus,* whose long narrow green leaves seem to tumble like water from a fountain. Chilean hazel bears white flowers which develop into cherry-like fruits; and the Chilean fire bush, *Embothrium coccineum*, gets its name from its bright red flowers.

Mr. McIlhenny had clearings opened along the Belgian Walk, letting the light in on beds of poppies and *Fothergilla* and, at this point, there is a small pond with a statue of a Hindu god.

After the pond, the Walk takes on the character of native woodland, with woodrush, ferns and mosses carpeting the ground. The canopy contains birch, oak, hazel and holly. There is a particularly mild microclimate in this spot which is ideal for the cultivation of tender species. Large-leaved

Fascicularia bicolor

rhododendrons - *R. protistum, R. mollyanum* and *R. macabeanum* - grow beneath the canopy, while *Fascicularia bicolor,* a relative of the pineapple normally seen in more southern climes, thrives on the left of the path.

Stop 10 There is a good view of the Pleasure Grounds from here. Around you are some southern beeches - *Nothofagus dombeyi, N. procera and N. cunninghamii* - and a fine native oak. Along the path you may notice the compact *Rhododendron yakushimanum* with tan-coloured underleaves.

The Walled Garden

Stop 11 At this point you leave the woodland of the Belgian Walk and enter a more domestic setting. The Walled Garden is laid out in the style of a French *jardin potager* or vegetable garden. When the Castle was a private residence, the box-edged beds provided fruit, vegetables and cut flowers. The herbaceous borders are planted with gaily-coloured summer-flowering species, including delphiniums, lupins, phlox, geraniums, irises and peonies. The garden cottage was, for many years, home to the head gardener, Matt Armour.

Stop 12 The fountain is a focal point in the Walled Garden. From here, an avenue of plum, pear and apple trees frames the view of the Orangerie, a conservatory built in 1958 to designs by Philippe Jullian and rebuilt in 1989. It is stocked with fragrant, colourful flowers, including highly-scented lemon geraniums.

The terraces in front of the Orangerie are furnished in an Italian manner. Plant-filled terra-cotta pots, box hedges clipped into corkscrew shapes and an assortment of seats and statuary add considerable charm to this restful setting.

Stop 13 The climate in Glenveagh is too wet for the larger roses, but not for the fragrant-scented shrub roses or rugosas, which flourish here in the Rose Garden. On the left behind the wall is a row of *Acer pseudoplatanus* 'Brilliantissimum', which are at their best in May. The wood-shingled gazebo provides a pleasant place to relax.

View Garden

Olearia macrodonta

Stop 14 You have now entered the View Garden, which offers a framed view of the Upper Glen and Lough Veagh. It provides a link between the formal elegance of the Gardens and the grandeur of the surrounding scenery. The plants in this garden are subdued in colour, with the brightest being a leafy evergreen called daisy bush, *Olearia macrodonta*, with *Cotoneaster horizontalis* and *Elaeagnus pungens*.

Stop 15 Beyond the circular lawn, a gate leads to the Viewpoint Trail (see p.121), with its oak groves and gushing streams. These natural habitats make a fine contrast with the man-made gardens. Before the gate, there are

Aran
Island
GLENVEAGH
NATIONAL
PARK
Kameiton
Burt Castle
Der

specimens of the native bird cherry, *Prunus padus,* growing on either side of the path. These were grown from seedlings collected locally.

Staying on the Garden Tour, you pass a selection of tall *Philadelphus* cultivars on the left. On your right, you can see *Magnolia wilsonii* and the early-flowering *Rhododendron* 'Shilsonii', distinguished by its plum-coloured bark. There is a 'white garden' here, complete with summer-house.

Beyond the exit and next to a blue cedar is a fine *Hoheria lyallii*, which produces a mass of white flowers in late summer. Beside it is the related *H. populnea*. Both are plentiful in the Gardens.

Crossing the avenue which leads up the Glen from the Castle, you pass through a gate to enter a series of small gardens situated by the lakeshore. You immediately come upon *Osmanthus heterophyllus* 'Myrtifolius', an attractive foliage plant with neat green leaves. Specimens of the hybrid *Rhododendron* 'Polar Bear', the latest-flowering rhododendron in the Gardens, and *Senecio hectoris* (with big daisy-like flowers) are cultivated here.

Stop 16 The Swiss Walk, laid out in 1954, is so called after a Swiss gardener named Brugger who planned it while assisting James Russell. Lodgepole and Scots pines form a canopy overhead, and to the left of the path a strawberry tree *Arbutus x andrachnoides* is hidden in the heavy shelter. This is a hybrid between the arbutus found naturally in parts of Ireland, including Killarney, and a related species found in Greece.

Stop 17 This point offers another fine view of Lough Veagh. When the wind sweeps down the valley, it is easy to appreciate the importance of the shelter-belts for the more tender plants. A collection of *Sorbus* and *Ilex* varieties is developing behind the seat. Groves of colourful, deciduous azaleas line the path, flowering in April/May. *Olearia x hastii* and *Senecio buchananii* are ideally suited to this exposed location.

Stop 18 The Italian Garden, created around 1958, is primarily a place of form and contrast rather than colour and is the most important formal element in the Gardens. Its rectangular lawn is lined by *Griselinia* hedges, in and against which are set Italian busts and statues imported from Florence, and old stone benches. The scene is framed at the far end by two variegated sycamores and to the side, by overhanging specimens of *Eucryphia (E. cordifolia* and *E. x nymansensis* 'Mount Usher') and other shrubs.

Follow the path by the Castle Terrace to see the old boat-house and swimming pool by the lake. The pool was heated by a boiler, and its changing booths and walls are turreted and battlemented to integrate with the castle. Across the lake, the enclosed woodland has been fenced to protect it from the unwanted attentions of deer, which were preventing its regeneration. A rich growth of young trees is now evident.

You have reached the end of the Garden Tour. If you make your way up to the bus yard, you will reach the spot where you began the tour. A great old Scots pine stands in the centre of the yard, where you can also admire Chilean lantern trees *Crinodendron hookerianum*, with their red, pendulous blossoms.

If you have time, you might like to visit the Castle tea rooms, which are open from Easter to September. There are fig trees and *Luma (Myrtus) apiculata* in the flag-yard outside, and hydrangeas and azaleas in ornamental terra-cotta pots.

The Italian Garden

Ramelton
Burt Castle
Aran Island
GLENVEAGH
NATIONAL
PARK
Der

The Landscape and Geology of Glenveagh

The basic ingredient of the Glenveagh landscape is rock - rock sculpted and shaped into hills and valleys and thinly covered in soil, vegetation and water. How the rock came into being and how it was moulded into its present shape is a story that challenges the human imagination on many levels.

To grasp fully the age of the rocks and the interminably slow processes that produced and shaped them, we need a special perspective on time; for the appearance of mankind is a very recent event in the history of the Earth, representing barely a billionth of the age of the Earth. The origin of the rock is rooted in the history of the Earth, which is approximately 4,600 million years old. During this long history, rock-building and rock-weathering processes have worked in parallel to shape the landscape. The corner of the planet that is now Glenveagh has experienced many cycles of uplift and erosion - the uplift resulting in towering mountains, erosion wearing the mountains down to a flat plain and seas have also washed over Glenveagh many times. At the heart of the rock-building process are great forces within the Earth's crust - forces great enough to move continents.

The Earth's continents and oceans rest on vast plates of solid rock and these plates float on less solid layers of rock (the mantle) beneath the crust. Molten rock from depths of around 300km continuously wells up between oceanic plates and solidifies, and this activity in the mantle steadily pushes the plates apart. As a result, over hundreds of millions of years, the continents have been pushed around the surface of the globe and oceans have opened up. Conversely, the plates have collided, closing existing oceans and forcing rock upwards to form mountain chains. At a local level, these events have helped produce the three main types of rock in Glenveagh: metamorphosed sedimentary rocks, that is sedimentary rocks altered by heat and pressure, granite and basalt.

Within the confines of Glenveagh National Park, granite and, to a lesser extent, basalt comprise most of the rock in view. However, the sedimentary rocks - best represented by the peaks of Errigal and Muckish just west of Glenveagh - came into being much earlier and any description of the Park's geology must begin with them.

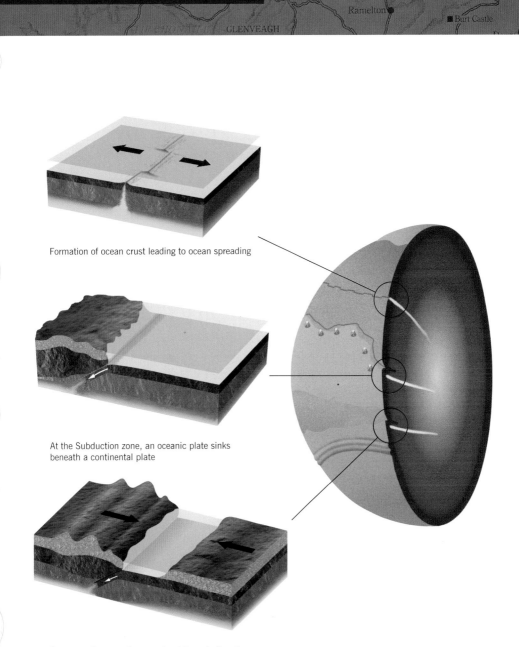

Formation of ocean crust leading to ocean spreading

At the Subduction zone, an oceanic plate sinks
beneath a continental plate

An ocean closes as the oceanic plate underthrusts
beneath a continental plate.

Aran
Island

GLENVEAGH
NATIONAL
PARK

Burt Castle

Den

50

Errigal Mountain

The Sedimentary Rocks

Between 700-600 million years ago, the area that now corresponds to Glenveagh lay beneath the sea. A continent known to geologists as Laurentia lay to the north-west, and this is today represented in Ireland only by a mere fragment - Inishtrahull Island off the coast of Donegal. Rivers drained and eroded the continent and carried vast quantities of sand and mud into the margins of the sea. The material was deposited on the sea floor in thick layers or beds. Bedding is typical of sedimentary rocks and reflects periodic changes in the raw material deposited such as sand, silt or limy muds. The beds became compacted into solid rock of various kinds, including sandstones, siltstones, limestone and shales.

The sedimentary rocks of Donegal are known as the Dalradian rocks, named in 1891 by Sir Archibald Geikie, in reference to the old Celtic kingdom of Dalriada which, like the rock outcrop itself, embraced much of south-west Scotland and the north of Ireland. These rocks extend all the way from County Galway to Banffshire in Scotland.

Initially, when laid down, these sedimentary beds were horizontal, but they are clearly not so now. They have been folded and thrust upwards over one another and from them erosion has fashioned, in this part of Donegal, the well-known peaks of Errigal and Muckish, amongst others. The folding and compression was brought about by a cataclysmic collision.

The Caledonian Orogeny

Between 500 and 400 million years ago, a continent lying to the south-east moved towards the continent of Laurentia and the two collided. The line along which the colliding continents merged may be traced across Ireland from near Drogheda to the Shannon Estuary. That two ancient continents are indeed welded together is very difficult to see but fossils remain of distinct marine animal populations that evolved independently on the margins of the two continents, separated by an ancient ocean. These can be found entombed in the rocks on either side of this line.

The sedimentary rock beds which had been layed down on the earlier ocean floor were put under enormous pressure, squashed between two continents, and they responded by folding and uplifting. The heat and pressure generated by this folding metamorphosed the sedimentary rocks, turning them into mica schists, marbles and quartzites and Errigal and Muckish are composed of white quartzite, a hard and durable rock which resists weathering.

The collision of the Earth's plates producing belts of folded and thrusted rocks is known as 'orogenesis', from the Greek meaning 'mountain building'. Orogenies involve not only the uplifting of mountains, but also ocean loss and the making of granite. The history of this particular orogeny, called the Caledonian Orogeny, was first gleaned from the rocks of Scotland, known to the Romans as Caledonia. The folding and subsequent uplift attributed to the Caledonian Orogeny resulted in a great mountain chain extending all the way from Scandinavia through Scotland and Ireland to eastern North America.

The Main Donegal Granite

Some 400 million years ago, deep within the collision zone, rocks melted at depth and vast masses of molten magma were squeezed upwards into the sedimentary rock layers. Such rock melts or magmas produce igneous rocks: granites from the slow cooling of magma at depth, and basalts from rapid cooling of lava at the surface. In Scotland, there is some evidence that magma reached the surface, appearing as belching volcanoes. In Donegal vast masses of magma cooled at depths of 5-10 kilometres beneath the surface. They slowly cooled and hardened forming large subterranean intrusions of granite. The largest intrusion in this part of Ireland was the Main Donegal Granite, the outcrop of which covers 350 square kilometres and centres on Glenveagh. The Caledonian Orogeny also resulted in the much larger Leinster Granite, comprising most of the Dublin and Wicklow Mountains.

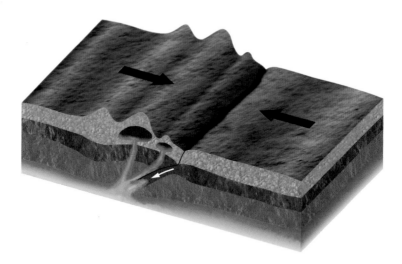

A continental plate underthrusts beneath another. As the crust is consumed, magma rises to form granite plutons which solidify below the surface in the mountain folds

The Caledonian mountains have long since been reduced by the the ceaseless action of wind, river-water and wave and several kilometres of rock thickness were removed so that the granite bodies were unroofed and exposed. Today only deeply-eroded remnants now remain and rocks that were once several kilometres below the surface are now exposed. The granite outcrops have responded differently to erosion than the sedimentary quartzites especially during glaciation so that, in Donegal, the rounded granite hills of Glenveagh now contrast sharply with the strongly defined quartzite peaks of the Errigal-Muckish range.

Some of the Dalradian sedimentary rocks that roofed the granite ended up as sandy deposits in another part of Donegal. They were compacted into rock called Old Red Sandstone, visible at Ballymastocker Bay near Portsalon on the Fanad Peninsula.

The Structure of Granite

Granite is a granular rock containing sparkling mica, white feldspar and glassy quartz. Individual mineral grains are typically a few millimetres in size. Though all granites contain the same minerals, they can look very different, e.g. grey or red, fine or coarse. Glenveagh granite is grey and medium in grain.

Here and there, small patches of rock, completely unlike the enclosing granite, can be found. These are xenoliths -'stranger stones' - small fragments ripped from the enclosing envelope of rock during granite intrusion. Such xenoliths, especially of quartzite and schist are dotted across the hills of Glenveagh, often in lines running north east to south west and representing septa or layers originally lying between separate sheet-like intrusions of granite.

Jointing of Granite

The Fracture Systems

Following the period of intense igneous activity, the rock crust was uplifted in response to regional forces connected with tectonic plate readjustments. The rocks responded by fracturing, producing an ordered array of rock joints. As is typical of granite, the joints are many and define a reasonably regular pattern, visible on any exposed granite.

The fracturing also produced a system of rock faults on a much larger scale, which sliced up the granite mass and the surrounding rock. The joint and fault fractures have largely determined the present topography of Glenveagh, providing the weak zones along which running water and ice have subsequently eroded the stream gullies and river valleys. The faults have a south-west to north-east orientation, as in the Glenveagh valley.

The valleys of Glenveagh and Gweebarra were eroded along the line of one of the main faults, the Gweebarra Fault. The rock walls on either side of the fault were wrenched sideways in respect of one another by some three kilometres, like two trains passing on a railway line.

The Gweebarra Fault. The rock walls were wrenched past each other by some three kilometres

There was much breaking and crushing of rocks in between. During the Ice Age, as we shall see later, glaciers occupied the fault and scoured out all the weakened rocks in their path, creating the two valleys.

Since the momentous geological events described above, north-west Ireland has suffered many uplifts, subsidences and incursions of the sea, of which little trace now exists in north-west Donegal. In fact, within the confines of the National Park, there are just two obvious relics of this long, post-Caledonian history; namely, the abundant basalt dykes and the widespread glacial phenomena.

The Basalt Dykes

Tree-filled gulley in an eroded Basalt dyke

Some 60-50 million years ago, as the North American and Eurasian continental plates were drifting apart and opening the North Atlantic Ocean, extensional forces affected the long-since solid granite. Rock fractures were opened, permitting the intrusion of volcanic basalt. The sheets of basalt cooled, forming what are known as basalt dykes, each 1-10 metres wide. Swarms of these dykes run right across north-west Ireland and across the Glenveagh mountains. The dykes are often evident as gullies caused by differential weathering. In the Poisoned Glen, almost every cleft and gully with a north-west to south-east orientation holds a basalt dyke. This feature is especially prominent on the cliff of the corrie head.

A rambler in these mountains should be warned that his compass needle may swing well away from magnetic north under the influence of the magnetic mineral ilmenite, dispersed within the basaltic rocks.

GLENVEAGH
NATIONAL
PARK

Aran
Island

Burt Castle

Derr

The Glaciation

About two million years ago, the world climate cooled and cold water currents from the Arctic swept into the Atlantic. The Ice Age had begun. During this period, the latest in geological history, the polar ice-caps advanced and retreated many times and ice built up on land-masses far from the poles.

Arctic weather gripped north-west Europe, and mountain ranges became centres of glacier growth. As the cold intensified, the glaciers expanded and merged, forming ice-sheets which covered the mountains and spread under their own weight. Their powerful erosive impact sculpted and shaped the landscape.

The freeze was not continuous and periods of glaciation alternated with periods of relative warmth. During the interglacial periods, average annual temperatures differed little from those of today and plants and animals of temperate climes were able to return to the country. Man, however, had yet to arrive in Europe for the first time.

Each successive glaciation re-worked the landscape, obliterating the effects of the one that preceded it. During the most recent glaciation - which lasted from 115,000 to 10,000 years ago - the mountains of Donegal formed a centre of ice accumulation. The resulting extensive ice-sheet flowed out over the surrounding countryside and prevented the Scottish ice-sheet from advancing further south than the Inishowen Peninsula. At the height of the last glaciation, the mountains were buried in ice.

The ice moved in all directions from a source high on the Donegal mountains. Clear evidence of the direction of ice movement is provided by striae - scratches made on rock by boulders carried within the ice, *roches moutonnées* which can best be translated from the French as 'rocks shaped like breaking waves', and the distribution of drumlins (egg-shaped hills of glacial debris) and erratics (lone rocks carried from distant sources and deposited by melting ice-sheets). The distribution of corries and U-valleys provide further evidence of ice collection and erosion. Today, many of the corries contain small upland lakes.

The 'U' shaped valley of Glenveagh

Glenveagh and the glen of Gweebarra provide excellent examples of the deep ice-scoured U-valleys along fault zones. They were both carved by glaciers following the south-west to north-east line of the Gweebarra Fault. The Glenveagh glacier originated at the head of the Glenveagh valley - beginning in a hollow or corrie carved by previous glaciations - and it flowed towards what is now the Park entrance. It cut deeply into the valley floor. Cliffs up to 200m high rise above the shores of Lough Veagh, which is 49m deep at its deepest point. This means that the glacier was at least 250m deep. Rocks and gravel carried within the glacier abraded the cliff-faces, leaving them smooth or 'pavemented'. The glacier flowed into Sheephaven Bay to the north.

A mountain saddle separated the Glenveagh glacier from the one in Gweebarra, which followed the same fault line in the opposite direction, towards Doochary. However, Glenveagh's corrie head was removed by backward erosion and the two glens became linearly linked.

Astelleen Waterfall

Glenveagh's high tributary valleys held smaller glaciers which flowed onto the surface of the U-valley glacier. When the ice melted, the tributaries were left 'hanging' above the U-valley and were drained by waterfalls or cascades. Several hanging valleys can be seen above Glenveagh, the best example being the Waterfall Glen. The hanging valleys are separated by spurs whose ends were removed by the U-valley glacier. These truncated spurs end in craggy precipices overhanging the U-valley.

As the Ice Age drew to a close, the Glenveagh valley glacier retreated in stages, melting back towards its corrie head. At each stage, its snout

GLENVEAGH
NATIONAL
PARK

Aran
Island

Kamenon

Burt Castle

Der

deposited rocks, gravel and sand in a semi-circular mound or moraine. One moraine spans the valley at the Visitor Centre. It extends into Derrylahan, where a tall plantation of Scots pines grows on the free-draining soil covering the glacial debris. A later moraine, including an outwash fan (a fan of sand and gravel deposited by meltwater from the snout of a glacier), spans the valley near the waterfall above the head of Lough Veagh. In addition, a lateral moraine (debris deposited along the edge of a glacier) skirts the north-east side of the glen, just beyond the end of Lough Veagh. Farther downstream, to the north of Glenveagh, glacial debris was moulded into the well-formed drumlins of the townlands of Drumlea and Drumnacarry.

A similar valley glacier must have occupied the upper reaches of the Calabber River on the north-west flank of the National Park. Looking across this broad, smooth-flanked valley from summits within the Park, there is a fine view of the steep scree-covered slopes of the Errigal-Muckish range. The screes of shattered boulders were created by freeze/thaw action and the avalanching of the resulting rock debris during the latest stage of the glaciation. In freeze/thaw action, water entering cracks in rock freezes and expands, splitting the rock.

The Poisoned Glen

The Poisoned Glen is the most perfect example of a glaciated feature within the Park. It held a major glacier that flowed out to Dunlewy. The steep face of its corrie head is flanked by pavemented walls, and the corrie bottom represents the relic of a glacial lake dammed by morainic deposits. The glen opens out into the Dunlewy Valley, which is banked with lateral moraines. Dunlewy's loughs are dammed by recessional moraines, of which the Cung is the most obvious.

The imprint of the last glaciation is still fresh on the Glenveagh landscape and there is no better part of County Donegal in which to view some of the features arising from glacial activity.

The Climate of Glenveagh

It has been said that there is no such thing as climate in Ireland, only weather! This is because the changes in conditions from day to day sometimes seem greater than the changes from one season to the next. Irish weather is dominated at all seasons by frontal depressions moving in from the Atlantic, with westerly winds bringing frontal bands of rain followed by blustery showers. Steady conditions associated with high atmospheric pressure are relatively infrequent.

All the mountains on the west coast have high rainfall because they catch the rain clouds associated with the frontal depressions. Glenveagh is no exception. Rainfall usually occurs in small amounts on many days in the year, unlike some parts of the world where rain comes in heavy falls on a few days only. The driest period in Glenveagh is usually from March to June.

Winter at Glenveagh

Clouds limit the amount of sunshine in Ireland to about one-third of what is theoretically possible. This effect is greatest in the north-west and greater among the hills than in lowlands or by the sea. The weather station in Glenties, which is not far from Glenveagh, averages only 5.5 hours of sunshine daily in June and less than one hour daily in December. Glenveagh experiences similar levels of sunshine.

The Atlantic Ocean, and the air masses moving in from it, give Ireland a climate with a fairly narrow range of temperatures - the winters are relatively mild and the summers are cool. However, average temperatures are lowest in northerly regions, both summer and winter. As a result, the growing season is significantly shorter than in the south, and mountainous areas like Glenveagh have significant snowfalls in winter despite their proximity to the west coast.

Ramelton
GLENVEAGH
NATIONAL
PARK
Aran
Island
Burt Castle
Derr

60

Habitats and Wildlife

Probable land bridges between Ireland and Britain

When the Ice Age ended 10,000 years ago, it left Glenveagh as a bare and rocky landscape. As temperatures rose and the environment for plant growth improved, grassland became established and a wide variety of animal species invaded. The colonists had their origins on the European mainland, to which Ireland and Britain remained connected until sea levels rose as the ice - cap melted. The grassland was gradually invaded by trees, and were it not for the arrival of human settlers, tree cover might still predominate in Glenveagh. However, the settlers removed much of the woodland and this paved the way for the development of blanket bog.

The plants and animals that found their way to Glenveagh - occasionally with a helping hand from human settlers - had to contend with the local climate. Those best adapted to it survived and stayed, though their very suitability to conditions in the north-west often limited their success elsewhere.

The plants and animals of Glenveagh therefore show adaptation to a late spring and a short cool summer and can endure high levels of rainfall and below average Irish temperatures. Many are confined to the north-west in Ireland. They form an interesting group, showing close affinities with the fauna and flora of Scotland's western seaboard, which experiences similar temperatures and rainfall.

The granite bed-rock and rugged, exposed topography put further limits on Glenveagh's plant and animal life. Granite weathers slowly to produce poor soils. In Glenveagh, the soils are waterlogged and covered in peat and the grazing is of low quality. The wildlife suited to these conditions is quite specialised. Numbers vary considerably with the seasons and remain low in general. Bird numbers peak in summer and then dwindle in the autumn when many birds leave for more hospitable winter quarters.

Man's impact on the Glenveagh environment has been relatively small and most of the area is in a semi-natural state. However, past human activities such as tree-felling, the grazing of livestock and the creation of a deer herd have had a lasting influence on its ecology.

Glenveagh's habitats can be very broadly described as hilltops and crags, bogland, broad-leaved woodland, grassland and freshwater. In the habitat accounts which follow, we take an imaginary journey from the bare, windswept summits to the more hospitable environs of the valley floor. We have to take some licence in this journey, as both the freshwater and bogland habitats span all zones.

Hilltops and Crags

The rocky precipices have always remained free of peat and many of the hilltops have been laid bare by peat erosion and weathering. As a result, the summits and crags resemble parts of the Arctic and lower Alps, being sparsely vegetated with shrubs, mosses and liverworts. The plants include some 'arctic-alpines', which were amongst the first species to colonise Glenveagh after the Ice Age. Examples include alpine club-moss, bearberry, silvery moss and dwarf willow.

GLENVEAGH
NATIONAL
PARK

Aran
Island

Kamelton

Burt Castle

Derr

62

Roseroot

Starry Saxifrage

Arctic-alpines are adapted to a short cool summer. Many lie prostrate or hug the ground to avoid wind damage and may need several growing seasons before they can flower or bear fruit. Some, such as the rare roseroot and starry saxifrage, which are less tolerant of exposure, are found in ravines and on sheltered rocky slopes, such as in the Poisoned Glen. Juniper is found commonly on the summits. It is an evergreen shrub of northern latitudes.

The hilltops support a meagre and specialised wildlife. Look for the hare, which may jump from under your feet. This hardy mammal can survive on a diet of mountain grasses and sedges, though it also occurs on lower ground. It is a race of the Arctic mountain hare, but unlike the race found in Scotland, its coat seldom turns white in winter.

Hare

Snow Bunting

No bird captures the character of the hilltops more evocatively than the golden plover. Its sweet, melancholy call as it watches from a stone or peat hummock follows the hill walker. As a breeding bird, this beautiful plover is now quite rare in Ireland, where it is confined to the north and west.

Flocks of snow buntings from the Arctic visit the rock-strewn summits in winter, while the elusive ring ouzel, a migratory thrush associated with rocky uplands, visits the higher gullies in summer. It is a challenge to find one.

Peregrine Falcon

One of the main predators on the hilltops is the peregrine falcon, which ranges widely in search of food, particularly woodpigeons. Peregrines nest on the cliffs choosing their nesting ledges with an eye to their inaccessibility and favouring south-facing cliffs for warmth and light. Every suitable cliff is occupied annually by a pair, though it is difficult to pin-point their eyries on the cliff faces.

Peregrines almost died out in Ireland in the 1960's as a result of widespread use of organochlorine pesticides. The poison accumulated in falcons that fed on contaminated birds and it left many infertile. Numbers dropped to below 60 pairs before a ban on the use of persistent pesticides enabled the peregrine population to make a slow but complete recovery.

Ravens, which also nest on the cliffs, are the scavengers of the mountains. They nest as early as February, a time of year when hard weather and scarcity of grazing claims the lives of many deer and carrion is at its most plentiful. The raven's loud croaking call is unmistakable and a visit to Glenveagh should be rewarded with a sighting.

Aran
Island

Ramelton

GLENVEAGH
NATIONAL
PARK

Burt Castle

Der

Upland Blanket Bog

Leaving the barren hilltops behind, we begin our descent to the valley floor, which takes us across upland blanket bog. This habitat, which today covers the greater part of Glenveagh, was preceded by forests of Scots pine and birch, giving way to oak, hazel and alder on the lower slopes. Today, it is difficult to believe that tree cover extended to the upper slopes, but the evidence of tree stumps in the bog reveals that it did, though the higher summits remained unforested. Remains of the ancient pines can be seen protruding from weathered peat on many hills in the park.

The main phase of blanket bog development occurred from 4,500 to 3,000 years ago, during the Bronze Age. The growth of the bog was apparently triggered by the tree-felling activities of Neolithic farmers. This exposed the ground, allowing it to become saturated by rain and leached of its plant nutrients or minerals. The impoverished waterlogged soils favoured the growth of blanket bog flora, and peat accumulated.

Exposed tree roots in blanket bog

As blanket bog spread across the hilltops, the pine forests dwindled and disappeared. The pine made at least one temporary come-back, however, though peat eventually won the day - most likely due to increasing rainfall. Pine forests died out throughout Ireland during this period, though it survived in some parts until at least 1,800 years ago. It is not certain that the pine disappeared altogether. There is a strand of opinion which holds that it survived in small numbers, as some pines found growing on Irish bogs today are not easily ascribed to imported stock and could be native.

Bogland Plants and Grazing Animals

The blanket bog is of the Atlantic or western type, which is found only in Ireland, Scotland and Wales. In Glenveagh, the underlying bed-rock is fissured with geological joints and fractures, which appear as clefts and gullies. Peat cover is uneven and of varying dampness and bed-rock is widely exposed. The result is a mosaic of blanket-bog vegetational types.

Bell Heather

Ling Heather

The drier patches are favoured by ling heather, bell heather, crowberry and blaeberry. The latter shrub, which has edible blue berries, is also known as bilberry or, in southern counties, *frochan*. Crowberry is an enigmatic species: in Glenveagh, it rarely occurs below 450m but it is found at sea level only 20km away.

Aran
Island

GLENVEAGH
NATIONAL
PARK

Burt Castle

Der

The damper patches of bog support wet grassland containing fescue, deer-grass, rushes *(Juncus effusus and J. conglomeratus)* and purple moor-grass or *Molinia,* whose large green blades are tipped with purple. Deer prefer the sweeter grasses and heather, which they search out, and this favours the growth of *Molinia,* which is particularly abundant in Glenveagh. Likewise, tough plants like mat grass and heath rush are prominent as deer find them inedible.

Sundew

Pale Butterwort

Plants which are adapted in very specialised ways to nutrient-poor environments are a feature of bogs. They are separated from the mineral soil by a layer of infertile peat and they survive by exploiting other sources of nutrients. These plants include the sundew and butterwort, both of which extract nutrients from insects trapped on their sticky leaves. The roots of bog myrtle host bacteria that can assimilate nitrogen from the air, and the heather hosts nitrogen-fixing fungi. Most of the bogland plants augment their nutrient supply with inputs from rainfall, and some, such as bog moss, depend exclusively on this source.

Female Red Grouse

Heather is a particularly important food plant on the bog, and red deer and red grouse depend on it. Red grouse nest in mature heather on the drier slopes and in gullies, and feed on young heather shoots. They form small coveys of up to half a dozen birds, which can burst noisily from cover, startling the hill walker.

Red deer and hare are the main grazing animals and the best place to look for them is often along the fertile grassy banks of streams. However, the most abundant animals are less easily detected - the small mammals, lizards, frogs, birds and invertebrates (such as insects and slugs) which live on the surface of the bog. Their total biomass (or weight) far exceeds that of the grazing animals and they make life possible for a variety of bogland predators.

Fox

Bogland Predators and their Prey

The fox is the commonest of the predators, though its stealthy behaviour makes it surprisingly inconspicuous. Foxes need somewhere dry to bed down and many locate their dens in boulder-fields. Confident of the safety of their cubs amongst the rocks, they go hunting for small mammals, nestlings, slugs, beetles and especially frogs which are particularly numerous in Glenveagh.

Badgers are closely associated with stream confluences in the high tributary valleys, where they build their setts in dry sandy banks. Though nocturnal by nature, they are rarely disturbed here and can be seen by day, especially in spring. They spend a lot of their time snuffling for beetles and insect larvae.

Lizard

The lizard, Ireland's only native reptile, is particularly plentiful in Glenveagh and is hunted by many predators. A rustle in the grass on sunny days may draw your attention, though it rarely allows passers-by a close look.

The sheer abundance of meadow pipits in Glenveagh is noteworthy. Most depart for the winter, although no one knows whether they move to low-lying ground in Ireland or migrate to Spain and Portugal. Skylarks have similar habits, nesting in grassy tussocks and also departing for the winter.

The keen-eyed kestrel, Ireland's commonest bird of prey, hovers over the bog in search of unwary birds, mice, shrews, frogs and lizards. The merlin is a more dashing falcon which hugs the contours to launch surprise attacks on small birds. It is given to long aerial chases of meadow pipits, its principal prey.

Male Hen Harrier

Visiting raptors include hen harriers - which like to quarter the slopes in search of prey - and buzzards, which soar in air thermals above the spurs of the main glen. The awesome golden eagle is a very rare visitor, though it once bred here in good numbers. Perhaps it will take advantage of the National Park's security and return to breed again.

Insect life is abundant on the blanket bog, and a number of day-flying moths are particularly visible. The northern eggar and fox moths, perhaps best known for their furry brown caterpillars, can be seen throughout the summer, while the colourful emperor moth, with big eye-spots, is on the wing in May and June. The latter depends on the nectar of heather for sustenance. All of these moths fall prey to the merlin.

The deer are compelled to take to the hilltops in summer by biting midges, pinhead-sized insects which rise out of the heather in swarms on calm days and seek out warm-blooded animals. The horsefly, or cleg, is equally annoying but less numerous.

Bog Pools

In bog pools, typical aquatic plants of these mineral-poor conditions include a bog moss known as 'drowned kittens', as well as bogbean, pondweed and the rootless bladderwort, a plant which for lack of other nutrients feeds on water fleas. The peaty surrounds of the pools typically hold black bog-rush and common reed, and white-beaked sedge also occurs.

In the pools, a variety of dragonflies pass through their nymphal stages, involving a series of skin moults and the development of wing buds. On their final moult, they emerge from the water as winged imagos. The four-spotted chaser appears in early summer and can be seen quartering the pools and bogland, hunting for small winged insects.

Beg Bean

Four Spotted Chaser Dragonfly

Dragonflies which appear in late summer include the common darter and black darter. The large, blue-and-black common hawker roams more widely over the bogland and will wander into the woods on lower ground.

The Lower Slopes

Bog Cotton on the Lower Slopes

The blanket bog takes on a different character as it nears the lower flatter ground of the sheltered valley floor. Bog-cotton, whose snow-white cotton tufts are often identified with Irish bogs, makes a bold statement on the wetter patches. Bog asphodel is probably the most visible flower as, having flowered, its stems turn a dark saffron colour which catches the eye; it was once exploited for a yellow dye. Other flowers found on the lower slopes include tormentil, milkwort and lesser spotted orchid; the latter is restricted to the west in Ireland.

Bog Asphodel

Cladonia

On the drier hummocks, notice the cross-leaved heath and the abundance of lichens, most noticeably *Cladonia floerkeana* which is tipped with the bright red blobs of the sporing heads. *Cladonia* colonises bare peat and is often a sign of overgrazing or fire damage.

Purple moor grass grows in large tussocks on lowlying patches of bog with fluctuating water levels. Travelling on foot across the purple moor grass fields is very tedious, no matter how easy it looks, and to lose your footing is to risk a soaking. While overgrazing results in peat erosion, moderate grazing pressure helps to maintain the diversity of plant life, and it benefits at least one species of bird - the wheatear-which shows a clear preference for closely-grazed sward.

Snipe nest on the lowlying bogland, where the male's courtship 'song' may be heard on still summer evenings. Stiffening its tail feathers, it dives through the air, producing a whirring sound known as 'drumming' - once heard, never forgotten. The snipe uses its exceptionally long bill to probe for worms and other invertebrates in soft ground. Its smaller relative, the jack snipe, is a winter visitor to Glenveagh from northern Europe.

Derrybeg Bog

There is an old, quaking bog located on the flats at the head of Lough Veagh. Called Derrybeg Bog, it contains four metres of accumulated peat and silt, representing a full 8,000 years of bog growth. Preserved within its peat and silt are pollen grains from plants that grew on and around the bog as it developed. By analysing the pollen found at different depths, it is possible to reconstruct the area's entire vegetational history. Analysis of a vertical core from Derrybeg Bog has provided important information on changes that took place in Glenveagh's landscape since the Ice Age.

Golden plover

The boglands south and east of Lough Barra are probably the most important peatlands in Donegal, not least because of the expanse of undisturbed and undeveloped land. As well as having a rich plant life, they are the breeding grounds for dunlin and golden plover and in winter are visited by Greenland white-fronted geese. This is a species which used to winter mainly on bogs but the geese have learned in recent times that intensively managed farm land offers richer feeding.

Woodland

Mullangore Woodland

The Park contains about 100 hectares of natural and semi-natural woodland. The largest continuous stretch is Mullangore Wood on the south-eastern shore of Lough Veagh, although several smaller remnants are found on the steep slopes of Glenveagh where the terrain is too precipitous for blanket bog growth. The woods are amongst the few stands of native timber left in Donegal.

They are dominated by oak and birch, with lesser amounts of rowan, holly, hazel, yew and aspen. Bird cherry is also present in Glenlack. Woods of this kind are called western oakwoods and occur principally in the uplands of Ireland, Scotland and Wales.

Oak Woodland

Oakwoods were formerly widespread in Ireland. Their destruction commenced with the advent of Neolithic cultivation about 5,000 years ago and continued until recent times. It is likely that no more than tiny fragments of truly natural oakwood remain anywhere in Ireland, and then only in places such as inaccessible cliffs and slopes.

Lesser twayblade

The denser areas of woodland are rich in plants adapted to moist and shady conditions. Mosses and ferns form lush green carpets on boulders and trees, and delicate filmy ferns sprout from the banks of moss. Golden-leaved saxifrage and liverworts cover the wetter rocks, and woodrush, wood sorrel and wood anemone abound on the woodland floor. A tiny orchid called the lesser twayblade occurs sparingly. Red deer find woodland plants particularly palatable and the woods are heavily grazed except where fences keep them out.

The woods are at their busiest in summer, when rising sap and fresh foliage provide plenty of food for animals and insects. A variety of migrant birds, including spotted flycatcher and chiffchaff, arrive from Africa in mid May, in time to exploit the summer abundance of insect life.

Spotted Flycatcher

Redstart

The dominant tree species can have an important bearing on the type of birds found in a wood. The oak attracts the wood warbler, a rare bird in Ireland but probably an annual visitor to Glenveagh. Arriving in mid May, the male claims his territory and advertises his presence to females by singing vigorously. The best way to locate one is to listen for its unique descending trill. The rarer redstart nests occasionally on the upper fringes of Mullangore Wood.

Woodland birds with a more catholic diet can remain all year round, variously feeding on nuts, seeds, berries, insects, earthworms and snails. Common residents include chaffinch, song thrush, woodpigeon and great tit. The scarcer treecreeper, resembling a small woodpecker, is able to extricate insect larvae from their winter hiding places in tree bark. Sparrow-hawks launch surprise attacks on the smaller songbirds and are adept at pursuing them through the trees. The beautifully-coloured jay is a recent colonist which first appeared in the woods in the 1980s. Its screeching call betrays its presence in the tree tops.

The woodcock is related to wading shorebirds but is uniquely adapted to woodland life. It uses its long bill to probe for worms in muddy leaf-litter, and its beautiful plumage blends in perfectly with a background of dead leaves. It is most easily seen in June when the male is 'roding' - a word which describes his habit of circling his territory, calling to attract a mate and ward off rivals. Woodcock numbers are augmented in winter by Scandinavian migrants which frequent the woods and lower heaths.

Conifers planted in parts of the main glen harbour some typical pinewood birds, including crossbill, siskin, goldcrest and coal tit. Crossbills, whose curious bills are adapted to prising seeds from pine cones, were first recorded breeding in Glenveagh in 1980. Irish coal tits are thought to form a distinct race as they appear to have a bigger bill and more sombre colouring than the continental race.

GLENVEAGH
NATIONAL
PARK

Aran
Island

Burt Castle

Derr

76

Field Mouse

Badgers and foxes are important predators in the woods, though both are more commonly seen on the open heath. Their prey includes a little-seen denizen of the woods, the long-tailed field mouse, and the cryptically-coloured woodcock.

Bats emerge from hibernation in early summer. By then, their insect prey is on the wing. Pipistrelle, whiskered bat and Leisler's bat occur in the woods around Glenveagh Castle, and Natterer's bat has also been seen elsewhere in the Park. Leisler's bat is Ireland's largest bat species, with a 30 cm. wing-span, and it is more widespread in Ireland than in the rest of Europe, where it is a threatened species. Its decline is attributed to the loss of suitable roosting sites, such as hollow trees and unsealed roof spaces, and to the use of toxic preservatives on building timber.

Autumn, the season of leaf fall, sees the fruits of many different fungi sprouting on the woodland floor. The fungi play an important role as decomposers of leaf litter and fallen timber. The symbiotic pairing of fungi and algae produces lichens, which coat rock surfaces and trees. Lichens are highly sensitive to air pollution, but some 200 species are found in Mullangore Wood alone, which testifies to the purity of Glenveagh's air.

Late autumn sees influxes of redwing and fieldfare to the woods. These thrushes from northern Europe strip the holly and rowan of their berries and in the process help to disperse their seeds through the woods.

Redwing

Holly Blue

A great variety of native insects live in the woods. The butterflies are perhaps the easiest to recognise: the speckled wood is found throughout the woods, whilst the holly blue - which is quite local in Ireland - is associated with the holly, its host plant. It appears in the woods in May.

Rivers and Lakes

Lough Veagh

Four major Donegal rivers rise in Glenveagh National Park: the Owencarrow, Leannan, Gweebarra and Clady. Their sources are dozens of rivulets and rills tumbling from pockets in the hills and from tiny lakes or lochans at all levels, but particularly on the higher plateau of the Derryveagh range. The waters unite into tributary streams which flow into the four main watercourses on lower ground. Lakes in the Park range from the small lochans, through medium -sized lakes such as Lough Nambraddan and Lough Inshagh, to the long, deep Lough Veagh, the main body of water in the Park. The areas from which the lakes collect their water, or the lake watersheds, all lie entirely within the Park boundary, making it possible to prevent their pollution.

The lakes all have acidic waters and low nutrient levels, and water plants grow sparingly. The most obvious is perhaps the July-flowering water lobelia, whose flowerheads rise above the water surface and break into pale mauve bloom. Restricted to the extreme west in Ireland, it appears in almost every lake in the Park. The lake-shore vegetation is typified by black sedge and rushes, including *Juncus effusus and J. acutiflorus.*

Water lobelia

The waters are clean and well-oxygenated and are particularly suitable for salmonid fish and eels. Most of the Park's lakes hold brown trout and eel. Lough Veagh has modest runs of salmon and sea trout as well as stocks of arctic charr. Like the salmon, the charr is seagoing in arctic and sub-arctic regions, but in western Europe it is confined to freshwater lakes, where it has remained since the Ice Age.

The 'land-locked' charr requires cold and unpolluted water and, with such a commodity now scarce in western Europe, it has become seriously endangered. Charr populations isolated in different lakes over the past 10,000 years have evolved slight differences. At one time, scientists believed there were six sub-species of charr in Ireland, most easily separated by colour, but now they consider them to be simply different races. Recent findings suggest that Glenveagh charr are significantly smaller than those in nearby Dunlewy Lake.

Otters follow the sea trout upstream in autumn and winter and are often seen on Lough Inshagh. They are most noticeable from February to June, and most easily detected at night, when animals maintain contact by calling to each other. A small number are resident. The smaller but similar North American mink has overtaken the otter in numbers but does not appear to affect the native animal in any way. The fish stocks also attract visiting heron and cormorant.

Red-throated Diver

Waterfowl are of major interest in Glenveagh and highlight the northern or Scottish connection. Visitors include red-throated diver and goosander, both of which are becoming more common in Scotland and spreading southwards. Lough Veagh has long been a haunt of the red-throated diver and it nests in small numbers in the Park's vicinity, its only Irish breeding centre. The divers feed in nearby coastal waters, and divers calling as they fly in from the sea to their nesting areas are an evocative feature of summer mornings in Glenveagh. Their courtship, conducted with deep wailing cries, can be observed on Lough Veagh in the spring.

The goosander, a diving duck, has bred in Glenveagh and at a Leinster site and a foothold in Ireland seems assured. It is closely related to the merganser, an Irish resident that nests in the Park from time to time. The osprey is an occasional visitor that would make a welcome addition to Glenveagh's breeding birds. Over 90 pairs now nest in Scotland, and ospreys migrating between Scotland and Africa are sighted in Ireland with increasing frequency.

Dipper

Common Sandpiper

The classic birds of upland watercourses, the dipper, common sandpiper and grey wagtail, all breed in the Park. The first indication of a dipper's presence is often its tinkling song, heard in early spring along mountain streams. Dippers can nest surprisingly high up in the hills. They have an unusual ability to walk underwater in search of food, which includes small crustaceans and

GLENVEAGH
NATIONAL
PARK

Aran
Island

Burt Castle

Der

Kamelton

insect larvae. A dark Irish race, *Cinclus cinclus hibernicus,* is recognised by science. The common sandpiper, which prefers the lakeshores to the streams, is a summer migrant from Africa and is largely confined to the west in Ireland. The grey wagtail also likes upland waters, though fast-flowing brooks anywhere will satisfy its needs. Though resident in Ireland, it is strictly a summer visitor to Glenveagh, apparently finding it too inhospitable in winter.

The common gull, which is not as common as its name suggests, has a western breeding distribution, both here and in Britain. In Glenveagh, it nests in small colonies on lake islands. A former colony at a hilltop lochan called Lough Naweeloge - from the Irish *Loch na bhFaoileog,* meaning lake of the seagulls - ceased to exist in the early 1980's, probably due to an increase in the number of peregrine falcons breeding locally. The colony was at an unusually high elevation.

Silted lakes with plenty of submerged vegetation play host to various wildfowl species in the winter, including whooper swan, teal and pochard. The whooper swan comes from breeding grounds in Iceland and sometimes small parties visit Glenveagh in the winter. It is particularly common in Donegal, the only Irish county where it is known to have bred. It feeds mainly on aquatic plants such as pondweed, which is fairly abundant in the Park, particularly in Lough Inshagh. The pochard feeds on water snails.

Large Red Damselfly

Beneath the surface of the lakes and streams, there is a thriving underworld of insect larvae, including the larvae of stoneflies, mayflies, midges, dragonflies and damselflies. The winged adults of damselflies display striking colouration. Damselflies associated with the Lough Veagh outflow - one of the richest sites in Glenveagh for freshwater insects - include the metallic-blue banded agrion, the large red damselfly, the common blue damselfly and the emerald damselfly, all of which fly in June-July. Bats may be seen skimming over the water surface at dusk in pursuit of insects.

Lough Nacally

The lowlying loughs on the eastern perimeter of the Park - Gartan, Akibbon and Nacally - are richer in nutrients and have much more emergent vegetation. Their heavier nutrient loads are mainly due to run-off from surrounding fertilised farmland. They support strikingly different breeding birds such as great crested grebe, little grebe, mute swan, coot and tufted duck. The fens and reedbeds at the lake edges hold water rail, grasshopper warbler and sedge warbler. The last two species migrate between West Africa and Ireland every summer.

Grassland and Scrub

Grassland and Scrub at Derrylahan

The 'wandering voice' of Wordsworth's verse, the cuckoo, is not really all that elusive. It is usually seen on a tree or pole on which it perches to sing. In Glenveagh, this usually means on the lower margins of the blanket bog where it gives way to arable land. This transitional zone, formerly of woodland

GLENVEAGH
NATIONAL
PARK

Aran
Island

Burt Castle

Derr

or heath, was cleared for farming and now comprises a man-made habitat, predominantly of grassland and scrub. It has its own distinct community of plants and animals.

This is the habitat around the Visitor Centre and, in Derrylahan, where the land is well-drained, grassy and fertile, was used in the past mainly to graze cattle. The very names of the plants in this habitat suggest an environment of pleasant pastures. The meadow grasses consist mainly of Yorkshire fog, bent grass, fescue, crested dog's-tail and vernal grass, while wild flowers such as cat's ear, foxglove, lady's smock and lady's bedstraw are common. Butterflies, particularly the small tortoiseshell and small copper, sip the flowers' nectar. The cinnabar moth is found associated with ragwort, a common yellow weed known locally as benweed. When cattle grazing was discontinued some years ago, the meadows were invaded by bracken, sedges and rushes.

Pygmy shrew

The rushy patches are good places to look for pygmy shrews, whose thin, almost inaudible squeaks are easily ignored. The pygmy shrew - Ireland's smallest mammal - is a hyperactive species, constantly searching for insects and grubs. Listen also for the reeling song of the grasshopper warbler in the rushy fields. This summer migrant is a skulking species, more often heard than seen.

Stoat

The meadows are a magnet for wildlife, and the predatory stoat takes every advantage of this. Keep an eye out for it along stony dykes and ditches in Derrylahan. A race of the stoat peculiar to Ireland is darker than the race on the island of Britain and is locally known as 'whitterit' in reference to its white throat.

Stonechat

The upper margins of the farmland tend to be colonised by bracken, willow and whin (known elsewhere as furze or gorse). Where these plants occur, they tend to attract stonechats and whinchats, small robin-like birds of open heath. The whinchat, a summer migrant, is inexplicably absent from many Irish heaths but occurs in every suitable area in Glenveagh, including young forestry plantations on the edge of the Park. Most are found near water, which tends to be another feature of their chosen habitat. The single-brooded green hairstreak butterfly appears in similar habitat for a brief period in May. Scrubland of hazel, birch and willow have also become established, and this attracts migrant willow and sedge warblers in summer. The mistle thrush, whose natural habitat is the woodland edge, nests in Derrylahan and similar areas, but ventures widely over the heaths in search of food.

The human manipulation of nature receives artistic expression in gardens, which provide a productive, if artificial, habitat for wildlife. The Gardens at Glenveagh Castle are a case in point. They are the only place in Glenveagh where the shrubbery-loving warbler, the blackcap, has been seen. Likewise, the planting of prickly heath which has escaped onto roadsides in the Park, attracts bullfinches, which feed on its big mauve berries. Magpies, which were absent from the west of Ireland until recently, have taken to visiting Glenveagh, where they feed on scraps from picnic tables.

Red Deer

A native herd of red deer formerly existed in North Donegal but was hunted to extinction by 1845. The present herd of some 500 deer is descended from introduced stock. In 1891, six deer were brought to Glenveagh from Lincolnshire by Cornelia Adair and, over the next 20 years, 170 were introduced from deer parks in England and Scotland and from collections in County Fermanagh, County Down, Powerscourt in County Wicklow and Dublin Zoo. Henry McIlhenny also added some fresh stock between 1939 and 1966.

A deer fence was completed in 1897 to enclose what was known as the Glenveagh Deer Forest. It is somewhat surprising that an area so devoid of trees should be called a 'forest' but the term derives from English feudal times, where areas of land, usually wooded, were set aside for hunting, principally by the King. When deer stalking with rifles became popular in Scotland in the middle of the 19th Century, the term 'deer forest' became applied to those areas of the landed estates on which deer were stalked and the term was also applied on estates in Ireland.

The deer fence still surrounds much of the Park although it has never been entirely impervious to the movement of deer and a large area of the country-side around Glenveagh has been re-populated by deer which escaped in the past. These have now spread as far afield as Killeter in County Fermanagh.

Deer Fence Repairs

The Glenveagh deer forest was managed as a private deer shoot by its former owners and the deer-stalking rights were leased annually. During the 1950's and 1960's, when detailed records were kept, 20-40 stags and 10-30 hinds (females) were shot each season. Deer-stalking ceased when Glenveagh became a National Park.

Red deer are the largest and most obvious wild animals in the Park and may be seen at any hour of the day, although they are most active at dawn and dusk. In summer, they frequent the hilltops, while winter, or periods of bad weather, finds them mostly on lower ground. For such a big animal, the red deer confines itself to a surprisingly small home range and recognisable individuals can be located again and again at the same spot.

Ramelton

■ Burt Castle

Derr

Aran
Island

GLENVEAGH
NATIONAL
PARK

86

A Stag Roars in the Rut

The 'rut' or mating season extends from mid September to mid November - the best time of year to watch the deer. Mature stags round up large harems of hinds and spend much energy keeping them from the attentions of rival males. The stags find little time to eat, but, oblivious to cold or hunger, they wallow in wet ground, covering themselves in mud, and bellow hoarsely, which is their way of throwing down the gauntlet to rivals. Posturing and displaying of antlers is frequently enough to deter challengers, but well-matched stags engage in fierce clashes, with much pushing and shoving to ascertain strength and conviction. The vanquished suffers little more than bruises and a crushed pride, though serious injuries and fatalities occur occasionally. After the rut, the stags and hinds separate and remain as discrete groups until the following year's rut.

The camouflaged calf

Calves are born in June and are carefully hidden in long grass during the weaning period, during which their speckled coats help to camouflage them. They remain out of sight until August, when the hinds, accompanied by their calves and two year-old offspring, join hind groups led by older, more experienced females. Hinds tend to occupy the most fertile areas, probably as an insurance against undernourishment during pregnancy and weaning. All the deer moult in late summer and their rufous pelage is replaced by a light-brown, shaggy winter coat.

The male offspring leave the family groups on reaching maturity (at about three years of age) and join stag groups. Such groups have occupied the same areas for decades, including Staghall Mountain, Dooish, Keamnacally and the Poisoned Glen. Every April, the stags shed their antlers and grow a new pair over the summer. By late August, their antlers are fully grown and hardened and the velvet has fallen off. Stag groups break up in advance of the rut.

A calf accompanies its mother

The herd in summer

Antlers in velvet, and almost full-grown

The stag in winter

GLENVEAGH
NATIONAL
PARK

Burt Castle

Aran
Island

88

Conservation and Mangement

The primary role of the National Park is to conserve the natural heritage of the area, including its plant and animal life. Though still in a semi-natural state, the Park has undergone some key changes in the past and human exploitation over the centuries has left its imprint on the wilderness. As we have seen, most of the woodlands were felled and the wolf and red deer were driven to extinction. The deer were at first replaced by domestic animals and then by introduced deer, whose numbers grew to unprecedented levels due to fencing and the absence of predators.

The system of checks and balances that confers stability on natural ecosystems was thus unwittingly undone, setting off a new struggle for dominance amongst the inhabitants. The conservation programme aims therefore to restore the Park habitats to their original state and to provide protection and freedom from disturbance to plants and animals so that they may thrive.

The introduction of alien elements in the past, and the removal of key species, created a situation which, if uncontrolled, would lead to a new ecological balance, one in which many of the Park's indigenous species might not figure and would become extinct. To protect the Park's indigenous species, the environment must therefore be artificially manipulated, or in short, managed for wildlife.

Rhododendron ponticum

The introduction of *Rhododendron ponticum,* for example, had repercussions which vividly illustrate the dangers of tampering with the natural order. This exotic shrub has no natural enemies in Glenveagh - nothing will eat it and it spread rapidly, choking areas of woodland with its dense growth. Eliminating it from the park is a conservation priority.

The conservation programme is also concerned with prevention - the prevention of fire, water pollution, disease and so on. In this context, the possibility of invasion by species from adjoining lands, which are not managed for conservation, has to be considered. The World Conservation Union (IUCN) recommends that land-use be regulated in lands surrounding a national park, and in the long term such a buffer zone is planned.

Red Deer

As the red deer no longer have a natural predator, there is always a danger that the Park might become overstocked with deer. A herd size of 450 is considered optimal for the Park, and in order to maintain deer numbers at this level, a proportion of the herd is culled annually.

Culling is vital to the health of the herd, and it also benefits the environment. At times of greater deer density in the past, the woodlands and blanket bog-land were subjected to severe grazing pressure, resulting in poor woodland regeneration and peat erosion.

Kerry Cattle

In spite of the need to reduce grazing, a small herd of Kerry cattle is kept in the Park. Unlike deer, who, with their narrow muzzles can select out the most palatable species of plant leaving the less palatable, cattle with their broad muzzles eat less selectively. They therefore help to improve the diversity of plant life by grazing down tussocks of purple moor grass. and restricting the spread of bracken by breaking it down by trampling. This allows other plants to colonize and by removing the competion of the less palatable species, allows the more tasty forms a better chance to flower and set seed.

Rhododendron

Rhododendron ponticum is an exotic shrub native to the Black Sea region and parts of Spain and Portugal. It was introduced to Glenveagh Gardens in the last century and soon spread to the adjoining woodlands and hillsides. Although attractive in bloom, it is a serious pest in Glenveagh as it grows densely, casting a heavy shadow over young trees and preventing woodland regeneration. Also, Rhododendron leaf litter alters soil chemistry, preventing a rapid return by native plants to areas cleared of Rhododendron.

Rhododendron clearance

Attempts are being made to eradicate Rhododendron by cutting and the application of herbicides. Clearance work is already at an advanced stage, but Rhododendron produces vast numbers of wind-distributed seeds and the soil throughout Glenveagh still holds a formidable Rhododendron seed bank. As a result, the eradication programme will have to be continued for the foreseeable future. Fortunately, some of Glenveagh's oakwoods have escaped Rhododendron infestation.

Oakwoods

A major programme is underway to save Glenveagh's surviving oakwoods, which are threatened by a combination of deer grazing and Rhododendron infestation. The programme excludes deer from selected areas to prevent over-grazing. This boosts the survival rate of tree seedlings and helps the woodland to regenerate. The woodland exclosure programme is complemented by red deer control and Rhododendron eradication measures.

Birch, rowan, hazel and holly saplings are all growing strongly within the exclosures and will in time form a natural understorey to the oak canopies. The fencing will be removed when the saplings have grown to a size capable of withstanding browsing.

Bogland

Bogs are sensitive habitats which can easily be destroyed. In the wider context, the activities most damaging to bogland ecosystems include drainage, afforestation, turf extraction and sheep-farming. These can change the nature of a bog irreversibly.

From the middle of the 17th century onwards, the Glenveagh bogs came under increasing pressure from grazing animals as farmers herded cattle, goats, pigs and sheep onto the hills. Heavy deer-stocking this century maintained the grazing pressure and resulted in visible erosion of peat. Some limited turf extraction and drainage also took place, but damage from these was minimal.

Now that domestic animals have been removed and deer numbers are being controlled, the bogland is on the road to recovery.

Ramelton
Burt Castle
Aran
Island
GLENVEAGH
NATIONAL
PARK
Der
92

Exploring the National Park

A number of the walking routes suitable for visitors are shown on the map. Each walk has a number of stops on it which contributes to an understanding of the character and natural environment of Glenveagh.

Except for the Derrylahan Trail and View Point Trails, which return to their starting points, the time indicated for each walk refers to the outward journey only. The Park bus service operates from Easter weekend to early November. It runs between the Visitor Centre and Glenveagh Castle and may be used to get to the start of some walks or for the return journey from the castle. There is no charge for this service.

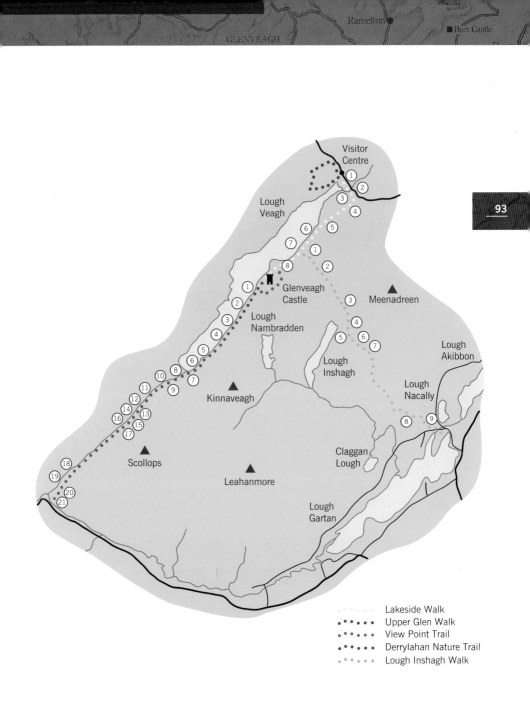

Ramelton
GLENVEAGH
Burt Castle

Visitor Centre

Lough Veagh

Glenveagh Castle

Meenadreen

Lough Nambradden

Lough Inshagh

Lough Akibbon

Lough Nacally

Kinnaveagh

Scollops

Leahanmore

Claggan Lough

Lough Gartan

⋯⋯ Lakeside Walk
•••• Upper Glen Walk
•••• View Point Trail
•••• Derrylahan Nature Trail
⋯⋯ Lough Inshagh Walk

GLENVEAGH
NATIONAL
PARK

Aran
Island

Burt Castle

Der

94

The Derrylahan Trail

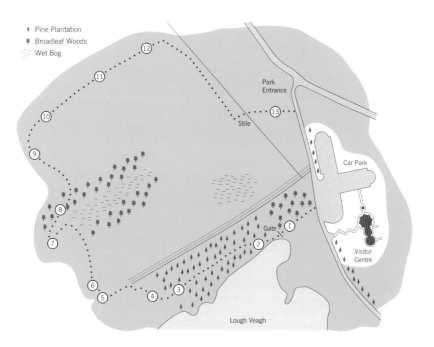

- ♠ Pine Plantation
- ♣ Broadleaf Woods
- ⚊⚊ Wet Bog

Park Entrance

Stile

Car Park

Gate

Visitor Centre

Lough Veagh

This attractive walk near the Visitor Centre is an ideal introduction to Glenveagh's natural environment. It passes through both native and planted woodlands, crosses a section of blanket bog and offers excellent views of the Glenveagh valley.

Length: 2km
Time required: Approx. 45 mins
Surface/gradient: An undulating, grassy track for much of its length. Not suitable for buggies or fashion footwear.

Stop 1 **Overgrown Field**

The overgrown field to your left was once a paddock where cows were kept by the former owners of Glenveagh. It is now returning to nature. Rushes, brambles and trees have reclaimed most of the field and in the fullness of time it should become densely wooded.

Several kinds of trees are already evident, including hawthorn, birch and rowan. Many birds, including parties of tits, forage for insects in the foliage. In summer, dragonflies skim over the field in pursuit of small winged insects, and rarer birds such as grasshopper warblers skulk in the undergrowth. The wildlife is better served by the scrub than by the bare pasture that preceded it because trees, shrubs and herbs offer a wider variety of food and shelter.

Sitka spruce and lodgepole pine are tightly spaced in the young plantation on the right and they monopolise the available light. For the moment, this prevents the development of a varied shrub layer and limits the plantation's species diversity.

Crossbill

Stop 2 **Pinewood**

This is a plantation of Scots pines planted about 1890. The pines attract a particular set of birds, including coal tit, goldcrest, siskin, treecreeper and crossbill. Of these only the crossbill - which feeds on the seeds in pine cones - is confined exclusively to coniferous woods, though siskin, goldcrest and coal tit prefer them to broad-leaved woods.

Stop 3 **Ravens**

If you examine the tree canopy high overhead, you may be able to pick out a raven's nest, consisting of a pile of loosely interwoven twigs. Ravens are the principal scavengers of the mountains and they range widely in search of deer carrion. This is at its most plentiful in late winter when many animal fatalities occur.

GLENVEAGH
NATIONAL
PARK

Aran
Island

Burt Castle

Der

Stop 4 **Holly and Rowan**

A naturally-developed pinewood typically has an upper canopy of tall pines, an understorey of smaller trees like holly, rowan, birch and hazel and a woodland-floor herb layer. The pinewood, despite its beginnings as a single-species plantation, is now growing in diversity to the benefit of wildlife.

The wood was fenced off some years ago and is not accessible to grazing deer. As a result, a dense undergrowth is developing. Many seedlings of holly and rowan are evident, but there are very few oak seedlings, which seems odd because all three species are found abundantly in the Park. However, there is a simple but eloquent explanation for this: in autumn, Glenveagh is visited by large flocks of redwings and fieldfares - migrant thrushes from continental Europe. They feed on the red berries of rowan and holly, and at night they roost in the pinewood tree-tops. Their droppings, containing the seeds of rowan and holly, fall to the ground below. Oak seeds (acorns), on the other hand, are rarely carried far from their point of origin.

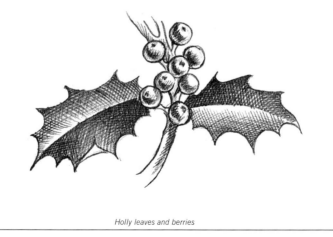

Holly leaves and berries

The next stop is the best point on the trail for seeing red deer. The quieter you approach, the better your chances of seeing some.

Stop 5 Glacial Moraine

The dry grassy ridge you are now standing on is part of a glacial moraine that was laid down during the last Ice Age. A glacial moraine is a semi-circular ridge of sand, gravel and rocks deposited at the melting snout of a glacier. It may be over a mile wide. Its topsoil is free-draining and fertile and was farmed in the past. Today it attracts grazing red deer in good numbers and their droppings of loose pellets litter the ground.

The movements of the deer are not always predictable, but many spend the summer on high ground, where they go to escape the attentions of biting insects. Winter, or periods of bad weather, find them using sheltered areas on lower ground. For the rest of the year, many follow a regular routine, moving uphill during the day to rest on higher ground - probably because it is safer to do so - and downhill in the evening to feed. They are most easily observed on low ground at dawn and dusk.

This part of Derrylahan (from the Irish *Doire Leathan*, meaning broad oak-wood) was originally well-wooded, but before the Famine (pre-1845) and in later times it was inhabited and cultivated. The re-growth of the wood has been hindered by grazing deer and the spread of bracken. In summer, the meadows are dotted with eyebright, lady's bedstraw and other colourful wild flowers, and stonechats and whinchats nest regularly.

Lady's bedstraw

GLENVEAGH
NATIONAL
PARK

Aran
Island

Burt Castle

Der

98

Stop 6 **Valley View**

This vantage point gives a fine view of the valley of Glenveagh. It is a classic U-shaped valley, gouged out of the landscape by glacial action during the Ice Age. Examples of every major habitat in the Park can be seen from this point - an upland river and lake system, oakwoods, grasslands and western blanket bog.

If you have binoculars with you, it is worth scanning the water around the islands for otters, red-throated divers and jumping trout and salmon. Donegal is currently the red-throated diver's most southerly breeding station; its main breeding grounds are further north in Scandinavia and Iceland.

Stop 7 **Marsh Insects**

This marshy hollow is favoured by damselflies and dragonflies, and you are certain to see some on sunny summer days. Damselflies are often brightly coloured and are butterfly-like in flight. Dragonflies are less colourful but are

strong fliers. They hunt all manner of small winged insects which feed or breed in the marsh.

Dragonflies need the warmth of the sun to fly and become torpid or inactive in cold weather. The principal dragonflies found here are the common hawker and the four-spotted chaser, while common damselflies include the large red damselfly and the common blue damselfly.

Iris

The marshy hollow is also favoured by butterflies, including green hairstreak, common blue and small white. Wild Irises grow abundantly in the marsh, together with bog myrtle - a low shrub with fragrant leaves - and hummocks of purple moor grass. The grass blades reveal signs of grazing by deer.

GLENVEAGH
NATIONAL
PARK

Aran
Island

Burt Castle

Derr

100

Sessile oak leaves and acorns

Stop 8 **Brogan's Wood**

You are standing beside Brogan's Wood, which is named after a family who lived here about a hundred years ago. The remains of their cottage lie nearer the lakeshore. Brogan's Wood is a remnant of the broad-leaved woodland that once covered Derrylahan. Though now sparsely wooded, it holds a good variety of native species, including hazel and blackthorn, both of which are scarce in Glenveagh, and the more plentiful oak, birch, aspen, rowan, hawthorn and holly.

In general, native trees support more types of living things than introduced trees because they evolved in tandem with local species and developed relationships over thousands of years. The oak, for example, plays host to over two hundred species of insects as well as many different kinds of lichens. One insect associated with the oak and also with holly is a butterfly called the holly blue, occasionally seen in Brogan's Wood.

Most of Derrylahan was cleared of trees in the past in order to cultivate the ground and provide firewood and building timber. Though these activities have long since ceased, the woodland has yet to regain its former size and density. Deer grazing on new tree seedlings have inhibited regeneration, as is evident from the stunted seedlings of oak and birch underfoot.

Deer slots

Stop 9 **Deer Tracks**

The trail at this point is used by deer travelling between the wood and the hill. Their hoof-prints or 'slots' can be clearly seen in muddy patches. Another sign of deer is the 'browse-line' on the ivy-covered tree trunks. Deer find ivy very tasty and eat every leaf they can reach, to a height of some two metres. Treecreepers like to nest in crevices behind the ivy stems.

Stop 10 **Mountain Blanket Bog**

Look back along the valley to see one of the finest views of Glenveagh. Bogland plant life is very specialised and consists of hardy plants, predominantly dwarf shrubs and sedges and a few grasses and mosses. Of the last, the bog moss or *Sphagnum* is the most important as it traps water like a sponge and impedes drainage. In the waterlogged environment of the bog, the remains of dead plants do not fully decay but accumulate in layers and slowly but gradually form peat. The process takes hundreds of years.

The type of bog found here is western blanket bog which is peculiar to Ireland and Britain and, as its name implies, covers large areas, sometimes whole regions. It is distinguished by the presence of black bog-rush and an abundance of purple moor grass, the grass which gives the hills of Glenveagh their bright green hue in summer.

Stop 11 **Bogland Life**

Plant nutrients are scarce on the bog because the mineral soil is covered by peat. This limits plant growth, but bogland plants are very good at conserving supplies. Some draw in nutrients from foliage which is dying off, while others tap more unusual sources. *Sphagnum* moss, for example, relies on nutrients found in dust and rain, including salt carried in from the sea, while sundew and butterwort trap insects on their sticky leaves and digest them.

Taller plants which take root on the surface of the bog include cross-leaved heath, black bog-rush and bog cotton, easily identified by its white cotton tufts in summer. Several colourful flowers can also be seen, including bog asphodel, lousewort, milkwort and tormentil. A bushy lichen called *Cladonia* favours the drier patches. It has bright red sporing heads.

Animals inhabiting the bog must overcome many problems to survive. For example, the soil is permanently waterlogged and there is little shelter from high winds. Frogs are one of the few permanent inhabitants. They like to sit in some convenient spot and wait for insects to come within reach. They catch them with their long sticky tongues.

Aran
Island

GLENVEAGH
NATIONAL
PARK

Burt Castle

Derr

It is not unusual to see hares and red deer on the bog, though the deer prefer to graze in drier places like woodland, where the pickings are richer. Birds which can take advantage of the bog include red grouse and meadow pipit. The latter is particularly common.

As it takes thousands of years for bogs to develop, it is important that some of Ireland's best remaining examples be conserved.

Cultivation Ridges

Stop 12 **Cultivation Ridges**

You are standing beside some old plots which were farmed in the 19th century. Their boundaries are covered in bracken and may be difficult to distinguish at first. They contain broad cultivation ridges or 'lazy beds' where potatoes were grown. The ridges are especially obvious in winter/early spring, when the vegetation is low.

Giant Boulder

Stop 13 **Giant Boulder**

This great boulder is an 'erratic', or a rock foreign to the area. It was transported within a moving ice-sheet during the Ice Age and deposited here along with other glacial debris. The rock is covered by crotal, a grey lichen used in the past for dying woollen garments.

After you cross the stile, notice the profusion of wild flowers on either side of the road. They include birdsfoot-trefoil, sheep's-bit, vetch and yellow rattle - all plants which clearly prefer the dry roadside fringes to the wet bog. They are annuals and will not be apparent in the winter months.

The Glen Walks

There are two consecutive Glen walks - one from the Visitor Centre to Glenveagh Castle, and the other from Glenveagh Castle to the end of the glen. Energetic walkers could combine the two. Together, the two walks run the entire length of the valley, linking the public roads at either end. The combined walk is 11km long. The 22km round trip may be completed in approximately 4-5 hours but take note: this is a long and tiring walk.

The Lakeside Walk Visitor Centre to Glenveagh Castle

This walk often produces sightings of red deer, particularly in winter when harsh weather drives deer down to low ground. In summer, deer are not usually seen before dusk. Scan your surroundings for the deer, as they tend to keep a safe distance between themselves and humans.

Length: 3km
Time required: Approx. 30 mins
Surface/gradient: A mostly flat, tarmacadamed road with a gravel path on one side. Please assist bus drivers and ensure your own safety by walking on the path.

Stop 1 **Bus Shelter**
The walk begins at the bus shelter below the Visitor Centre, from where there is a fine view of the Glenveagh valley. It is a classic U-shaped valley which was created by a major glacier during the Ice Age.

The stop is on a glacial moraine, which consists of boulder clay that was deposited by the melting snout of the valley glacier. The moraine forms the hill on which the Visitor Centre was built and it blocks the end of the lake, forcing the lake outflow to take a circuitous route around it.

Turn left and head down towards the river. Just before you reach Glenveagh Bridge (Stop 2), you pass some old farm buildings on your left. The former owners of Glenveagh Castle ran a small dairy farm here.

Stop 2 Glenveagh Bridge

This old stone bridge carries the former main road past Glenveagh; it has been superseded by the Glenveagh By-Pass. The broad-arrow benchmark on the bridge parapet (upstream side) provides a permanent reference point for Ordnance Survey mapping work.

The Owencarrow River, flowing under Glenveagh Bridge, drains Lough Veagh. The lake has healthy stocks of wild salmon and sea trout. You may be able to see some in the river, particularly in November/December when they spawn and lay their eggs in the gravel beds. When Glenveagh was a private estate, the fishery was managed and developed for fly-fishing and was stocked with fry from a primitive fish hatchery upstream of the lake. On summer evenings, look for Daubenton's bats skimming the water surface in search of insects, and pipistrelle bats, which prefer to hunt at tree level. With luck, you may also see an otter. Royal fern grows in clumps by the river. In Ireland, this is largely confined to western counties.

The house by the bridge is a former police barracks which was built by the estate's first owner, John George Adair, to protect his property. It later became the Estate Agent's House and was enlarged twice in this century.

Glenveagh Bridge and house

Stop 3 **Conifer Plantation**

This mixed plantation of lodgepole pine and sitka spruce was planted as a shelter-belt for the Estate Agent's House. It provides good nesting habitat for siskins and woodcock. Crossbills occur regularly and probably nest in the area. Beyond the plantation, you pass some modern buildings on your right, set in from the road. This is the administrative hub of the Park and includes offices, research facilities, workshops, student accommodation and stores.

Stop 4 **Entrance Gates**

The old entrance gates have stags' heads on their posts, with antlers from red deer shot on the estate. Deer-stalking was introduced to Glenveagh by Mrs. Cornelia Adair, who owned the estate from 1885 to 1921. She modelled it on the hunting estates of Scotland where the upper classes traditionally indulged their passion for field sports, and indeed still do. She stocked Glenveagh with red deer and also started a duck-shoot and developed the game-fishing. Wild stocks of snipe, woodcock and hare added variety to the shooting. Mrs. Adair became a society hostess of note and her house parties included many members of the British establishment.

Entrance Gates

Aran
Island

GLENVEAGH
NATIONAL
PARK

Burt Castle

De

The gate lodge to the right is one of a number that guarded the estate's entry points. Passing through the gates, you can see a weather station in a fenced compound to your left, set in from the road. It is one of the wetter stations in Ireland. The weather readings are taken by park rangers and passed on to the Meteorological Service.

An area of intact bog with its associated plant communities lies between here and the lake. It is known as Brady's Bog after the family who have lived at the gate lodge since the 1930's.

Stop 5 The Black Bush

This area is called the Black Bush after the gnarled, wind-sculpted oak tree by the side of the road. Despite its small size, it is undoubtedly very old. Across the lake from the Black Bush is an area called Derrylahan (from the Irish *Doire Leathan,* meaning broad oakwood). As its name implies, it was formerly well-wooded, but today only remnants of the original oakwood remain. In previous centuries, farmers felled its trees for timber and cleared the ground for cultivation. Bracken, which is associated with fertile soil, grows densely where the land was once tilled. It is worth scanning Derrylahan for red deer. The deer habitually move downhill to graze at dusk and move back uphill after dawn.

The Black Bush

The near end of Lough Veagh is shallow and has several small islands. As they are rarely visited by grazing deer - though deer can and do swim - the islands are thickly vegetated with small trees and shrubs. Common gulls, common sandpipers and red-breasted mergansers nest in the safety of the islands.

Some 300m further along the road is a lone whitebeam tree amongst the birch. It is readily identified from the silvery underside to its leaves. Five closely-related species of whitebeam occur in Ireland. The one found in Glenveagh - *Sorbus rupicola* - is relatively rare. There are only a few specimens in the Park, scattered around the rocky shores of Lough Veagh.

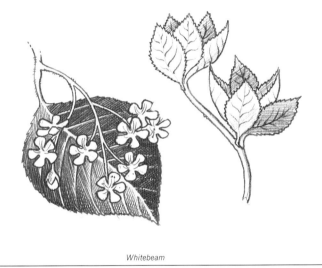

Whitebeam

Stop 6 **Woodland Enclosure**

The partially wooded hillside to your left is fenced to exclude deer and has been cleared of *Rhododendron*. These actions are designed to restore and extend the enclosed woodland, which was threatened by a combination of grazing and *Rhododendron* infestation. Relict woodlands respond well to such management practices.

Stop 7 Lough Inshagh Road

Note: The Lough Inshagh Walk begins at this junction and leads to Gartan, just east of the Park. It passes above Lough Inshagh, a remote mountain lake. Stay on the Lakeside Walk to reach Glenveagh Castle.

The Lough Inshagh Road, originally served as a shortcut from Glenveagh Castle to Churchhill, from where a train could be taken eastwards to Letterkenny or westwards to Burtonport. The Londonderry and Lough Swilly Railway Company opened a narrow-gauge railway line between Letterkenny and Burtonport in 1903. The service ran for 38 years before closing in 1941. In Mrs. Adair's time, the journey to the station was negotiated by pony and trap, then the most common method of private transport besides horse-riding.

In the absence of motorised vehicles the glen was unusually quiet and peaceful, an atmosphere heightened by the sombre mountains rising steeply on either side. Visitors can still savour this atmosphere as the Park is closed to private motorists. The parallels that Mrs. Adair saw between Glenveagh and the great glens of Scotland are not lost on the observant walker.

Stop 8 Duck Pond

This is a small artificial pond where mallard were reared for the purposes of a duck-shoot. It is now disused, but in its derelict state it attracts wild mallard and teal. A species of fly new to science was discovered here in 1987.

A woodland exclosure can be seen on the far side of the lake. The new growth within it differs markedly in colour from the vegetation outside, particularly in winter. The difference is explained by the impact of deer on the vegetation outside. The hill beyond and to the right of the woodland is frequented by up to 40 deer in summer. They can often be seen with the aid of strong binoculars.

Glenveagh Castle is picturesquely situated on a natural promontory. The location is most suitable for a fortified keep, but the castle - built in the 19th century - merely feigns a defensive role. The tall Scots pines lining the avenue are part of a shelter-belt which protects exotic plants within Glenveagh Gardens. A pair of somewhat imperious eagles embellishes the gate posts at the entrance to the castle grounds.

You have now reached the end of the Lakeside Walk. During the holiday season, which extends from Easter weekend until early November, visitors may sample a variety of attractions at Glenveagh Castle. These include a guided tour of the castle, a tour of Glenveagh Gardens, and an audio-visual display covering the history and traditions of Glenveagh and its hinterland. Refreshments are available in the tea-rooms.

There is also a short trail to a viewing point above Glenveagh Gardens, (see page 121) offering a panoramic view of the Glenveagh valley. It may be walked at any time of the year.

Glenveagh Castle

The Upper Glen Walk Glenveagh Castle to Upper Glen

This walk is the natural extension of the Lakeside Walk. It follows the shortest and most easily negotiated natural route through the Derryveagh Mountains. However, before the glen road was built, the route was so rocky and densely wooded as to be virtually impassable. Old settlements, now derelict, and native oak woodland can be seen along the walk, and there is a good chance of red deer sightings.

Length: 8km
Time required: Approx. 2 hrs.
Surface/gradient: A mostly flat dirt road for five kilometres, rising gently over the last 3km.

Stop 1 **Sawmill**
The estate formerly put windfall trees to use for fencing, carpentry and the manufacture of furniture. The timber was processed at this old sawmill,

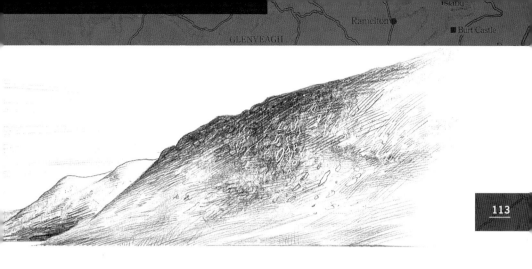

which is no longer in use. The Park philosophy is now to allow fallen timber to remain where it has fallen. This then provides habitat for the myriads of invertebrate species which feed on the decaying wood, further decomposing it and returning the nutrients of which it is composed to the soil.

Stop 2 The Long Hollow

From this point, there is a good view of the ancient oakwoods on the slopes of Farscollop, some distance ahead. Glenveagh's oakwoods are confined to steep rocky slopes in the central valley, where they are sheltered from the prevailing westerly winds. The trees are mainly sessile oak and birch, with lesser numbers of holly, rowan, yew and aspen.

Sessile oakwoods are closely associated with the poorer soils in the uplands of Ireland, Scotland and Wales. In Ireland, they are mainly confined to remote valleys with steep rocky slopes that have escaped cultivation.

GLENVEAGH
NATIONAL
PARK

Aran
Island

Burt Castle

114

Stop 3 **Aspen Trees**

A number of aspen trees can be seen here by the roadside. Aspen is most obvious in the woods in autumn, when its leaves turn a bright yellow. It is typically found on wet ground near lakes and streams. It is often called the "trembling aspen" because its broad green leaves on long, flattened stalks are moved by the gentlest of breezes; this is a special adaptation for shedding excess water.

Aspen leaf

The cliffs on the far side of the lake were moulded by the valley glacier during the Ice Age and were left relatively smooth and sheer. Being so precipitous, they provide safe nesting sites for ravens and a pair takes up residence there every summer. A scarce mountain thrush, the ring ouzel, nests in small numbers in the gullies. The slopes beneath the cliffs offer shelter and good grazing for deer, and it is a traditional haunt for stags in winter.

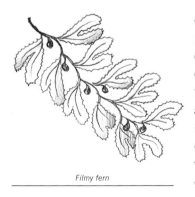

Filmy fern

Stop 4 **Filmy Ferns**

The bank by the roadside is densely covered in mosses and ferns. Notice the profusion of tiny filmy ferns, which are common in Ireland's moist western oakwoods but rare elsewhere, as well as the much larger hard fern (*Blechnum spicant*) Lough Veagh is at its deepest (49m) opposite this stop. Its surprising depth reflects the steepness of the valley sides and testifies to the scouring effect of the valley glacier.

Stop 5 **Mullangore Wood**

To your left is the best-preserved stand of natural oakwood in Glenveagh. Part of it has been fenced to exclude deer as their intensive grazing impedes woodland regeneration. As you can see, the woodland within the exclosure is developing a dense undergrowth, while the flora outside it is still closely-cropped, particularly between the road and the lakeshore, where the grazing is good.

Oak, birch and hazel saplings and bramble and blaeberry bushes have all responded well to the removal of grazing pressure, as have the woodrush and grasses carpeting the woodland floor. When the new saplings are tall enough to withstand browsing, the fence will be removed.

Yew trees are a natural constituent of Irish oakwoods and several examples can be seen on both sides of the road. Keep an eye out for jay, a colourful bird which recently colonised the woodland. Many dragonflies - especially the common hawker - and the speckled wood butterfly are seen in the glades in summer.

Stop 6 **Scots Pines**

The tall Scots pines by the lakeshore have all the appearance of self-sown trees but in fact are the remaining trees of an old plantation. They were spared for aesthetic reasons, whilst the rest were felled for timber. It seems likely that the promontory was cleared of natural woodland prior to its planting and that deer grazing has so far prevented the woodland's return.

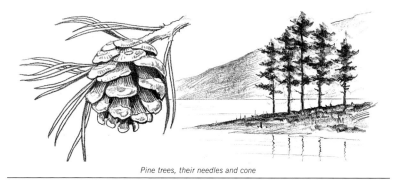

Pine trees, their needles and cone

GLENVEAGH NATIONAL PARK

Aran Island

Kamelton

Burt Castle

Derr

116

Stop 7 **The Beach**

The golden sand on the beach consists of peat-stained quartz particles, weathered from local bed-rock and washed down to the lake by mountain streams. The water-plant growing abundantly in the lake shallows is lake pondweed, or *Potamogeton*. Small groups of whooper swans come here to feed on it in winter.

Stop 8 **The Fishing Hut**

This hut was built to shelter anglers from the rain and provide a place to eat in bad weather. Peregrine falcons nest on the cliff face opposite the hut in summer. Their harsh mewing calls are often the first indication of their presence.

Derrybeg Bog stretches from the end of Lough Veagh to below the foot of the waterfall. Pollen grains from Glenveagh's vegetation over the last 8,000 years are preserved in its four metres of peat and silt. The pollen sequence provides a useful record of Glenveagh's vegetational history.

Fishing hut

Stop 9 **The Bridle Path**

The Bridle Path leads up through the woods to Glenlack and peters out on the open mountain. It was originally built to facilitate the stalking ponies which deer-stalkers used to carry their kills down from the mountain. There is a fine view of the glen from a point 800 metres up the path known as 'Mrs Adair's Seat'. You might like to make a detour to see it.

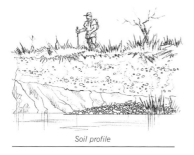

Soil profile

Stop 10 **Soil Profile**

Leaving the woodland behind, the road passes a small footbridge. The exposed river bank to the right throws some light on the history of sediment accumulation in this area. Several distinct layers of sediment can be made out, each laid down at different times and under different circumstances. One layer contains gravel deposits of river origin. It overlies a layer of red earth called an iron pan, which is impermeable to water and arrests the mineral iron leached out of the overlying soil. The pan caused water-logging of the soil and led to peat formation.

Stop 11 **The Astelleen Waterfall**

The waterfall is 215 metres high. It is usually quite humble but becomes a raging torrent immediately after heavy rain. The reason that the flow increases so rapidly is that the catchment area is thin-soiled and rocky and can only absorb a fraction of the rainwater.

Fish hatchery

Stop 12 **Stalking Hut**

The stalking hut was a resting place for weary hunters returning from the hill. The shooting party would sip hot drinks or dry themselves in front of the fire while awaiting transport back to the castle with their day's bag. It was also customary for house-parties to picnic at the hut, where they would be served a fine lunch by castle staff. The estate ran a primitive fish hatchery on the river here. Notice the steps or weirs which were built to provide pools for salmon.

GLENVEAGH
NATIONAL
PARK

Aran
Island

Burt Castle

Derr

Stop 13 **Walled Paddock**

The walled paddock on the left originally contained a vegetable garden for estate staff who lived here until the 1920's. It was also used to hold red deer prior to their release onto the estate. The deer were a natural addition to Glenveagh's fauna as a native herd existed in the area until the early 19th century. Native red deer are still found in Killarney, Co. Kerry. Some have been moved to other locations in the country to establish new herds of native stock.

Stop 14 **Glenveagh Cottage**

The ruins of several stone cottages and outhouses lie to the left of the trail. One was Glenveagh Cottage, where the estate's first owner, John George Adair, lived before he completed Glenveagh Castle. He probably renovated or extended an existing cottage for his own use. The head of the Mac Suibhne (Sweeney) clan is said to have lived here in the early 19th Century.

After Adair moved into the castle, the cottages were occupied by the estate agent and by workers and servants who ran a farm and laundry here. It was a hive of activity up to about 1918. The cottages were abandoned when Mrs. Adair began to spend an increasing amount of her time in England and fewer estate staff were required.

Some landscaping was carried out around the homestead. Old walls and paths are visible and there are mature ash, beech, Scots pine and sycamore on the lawns and roadside. Beech and sycamore are not native to Ireland, though they are long established in most parts of the country. However, they are frequently associated with parkland estates and the Adairs may have had this in mind when landscaping the site.

Stop 15 **The Slopes of Farscollop**

It was on Farscollop, the steep-sided mountain to your left, that Adair's steward, James Murray, was murdered in 1860, an act which led to the Derryveagh evictions. The mountain and the glen are much favoured by female red deer (hinds), especially in winter. By day, they are usually found on the steep slopes above the path, while in the evening they descend to the riverside to graze. It was not unusual for deer-stalking guides to bring their less nimble charges to Farscollop, where little climbing was necessary and a kill could virtually be guaranteed.

Stop 16 The Holly wood
Though consisting almost exclusively of holly trees, the sparse woodland on your left is not a true holly wood but is merely the surviving understorey of a former oak woodland. Such 'holly woods' are not unusual in Ireland.

Stop 17 Dohertys' Cottages
The wallsteads between the path and the stream are the ruins of 19th century cottages where a family called Doherty lived. The Dohertys were subsistence farmers who depended on potatoes for existence. Three stone buildings can be made out - one is probably a cattle byre or shed. Also evident is a kitchen garden and a tiny field system with cultivation ridges. A stand of bracken corresponds roughly to the original field.

Stop 18 Mulroney's Wood
The patch of oak woodland on the far side of the stream is called Mulroney's Wood after a family who lived in this area. The wood was almost certainly more extensive in the past, though we know from old maps that it was already greatly reduced by the time of the potato famine in the mid 1840s.

Purple moor grass grows in dense hummocks below the wood. Deer feed heavily on this grass in summer and eat its root-stocks in winter. The uprooted root-stocks are a common sight in late winter and often puzzle the uninitiated.

Mulroney's Wood

Stop 19 **Old Bridle Path**

This stop marks the start of an old and overgrown bridle path which crosses the stream and zig-zags up the far slope. After it disappears from view, it crosses a high mountain pass on Crockballaghgeeha (from the Irish *Cnoc Bealach Gaoithe,* meaning the hill of the windy way). The pass leads to the Poisoned Glen and the village of Dunlewy on the western edge of Glenveagh. It is difficult to imagine it today, but it was once used regularly by local people making their way to and from Dunlewy. In more recent times, after famine and emigration depopulated the area, the bridle path was used by deer-stalkers.

Stop 20 **Deer Fence**

The deer fence, built on Mrs. Adair's instructions in the 1890's, runs for 45km around the perimeter of the old Glenveagh Deer Forest. It is maintained by the Park staff, the better to manage the 500 or so deer within the Park boundaries. It also plays a useful role in keeping sheep out of the Park.

Stop 21 **County Road**

The first family to be evicted from Glenveagh in 1861 lived in this remote corner of the estate, called Gweebarra. The valley of Gweebarra lies straight ahead and has the same orientation as the valley of Glenveagh. Both held major glaciers during the Ice Age. The glaciers moved in opposite directions, one flowing south-westwards to Doochary and the other north-eastwards to Carrigart and Sheephaven Bay. At one time there was an arrête (a knife-edged ridge) between the two valleys but it was removed by backwards erosion of Glenveagh's corrie head. You are standing on all that is left of that ridge.

You have now reached the end of the Upper Glen Walk. If you have not arranged to be picked up here, you should retrace your steps to the castle. If you have transport, turn left to return to the Visitor Centre via Churchhill, or turn right for the village of Doochary.

The View-Point Trail

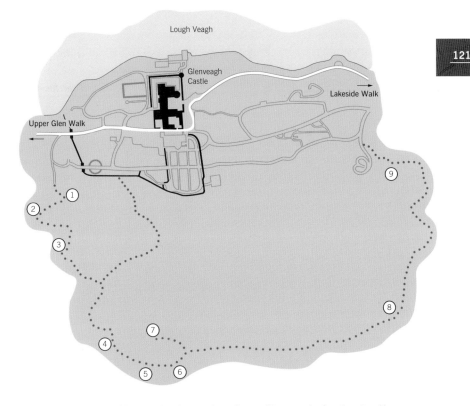

Lough Veagh

Glenveagh Castle

Lakeside Walk

Upper Glen Walk

This is a short trail to a viewing point above Glenveagh Castle. It offers a stunning panoramic view of the Glenveagh valley. The valley was hewn out during the Ice Age and many of the classic features of glaciation are clearly evident. The trail descends by way of the Castle Gardens.

Length: 1km
Time required: Approx. 40 mins
Surface/gradient: A stony path with a short but steep ascent to a viewing point above Glenveagh Castle. The path returns to the Garden by another steep route.

Stop 1 **Granite Seat**

As you begin this walk, you will notice that a fairly steep climb is in store - you may even be tempted to sit down here before going any further! It may also strike you that the valley slopes are well-wooded whilst the mountains are treeless, though covered in peat. The reasons for this are diverse: peat cannot accumulate on very steep slopes as it is wet and will slide away under its own weight. Broad-leaved woodland, on the other hand, is strongly rooted in the ground. It also requires shelter from high winds and will not flourish on high, exposed ground.

The bed-rock of Glenveagh consists mainly of granite. Donegal granite can be distinguished from other Irish granites by its fine grain and dark grey colour. Like all granites, it weathers slowly to produce an acidic mineral soil that is poor in plant nutrients.

Granite seat

Bog myrtle

Stop 2 **Mountain Vegetation**

This open patch of wet heath is fairly typical of the vegetation grazed by the red deer in the valley. Notice the clumps of purple moor grass, whose broad green leaves are tipped with purple, and the bog myrtle and heather growing in their midst. These plants are not very nutritious and the deer must feed intensively to obtain the calories they need. They also browse the leaves of trees, where they can reach them, and search the woodland floor for tree seedlings and other plants.

Stop 3 **Stunted Trees**

The oak, holly and birch trees to the left of the trail are quite stunted as exposure to the wind at this site has inhibited their growth. New buds develop best on the sheltered side ot the tree, so the trees grow in a lopsided 'windswept' shape. The woodlands reach their full potential in more sheltered parts of the valley.

Stop 4 **Stream**

At this point, the trail crosses a small stream, one of hundreds draining the slopes of Glenveagh. The streams rise in spate within minutes of a heavy shower as Glenveagh's thin, waterlogged soils can only absorb a fraction of the rainwater.

Stop 5 **Granite Blocks**

These granite blocks were created by the weathering and decay of the rocks that surrounded them. The rotted material fell away, exposing the upstanding blocks of solid rock. In time, they too will be weathered away.

The well-drained peaty soil surrounding the granite blocks is particularly suitable for heather, which grows here in thick clumps. Tall heather is ideal nesting habitat for red grouse, which feed on young heather shoots. Grouse are found in several parts of Glenveagh.

Granite blocks

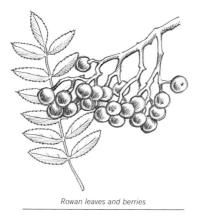

Rowan leaves and berries

Stop 6 **Birch Trees**

Birch trees dominate the upper limits of the woodland, or the tree-line. This is normal with oakwoods, as birch is hardier than the oak and tolerates a greater degree of cold. There is also some rowan or mountain ash here, most easily distinguished by its bright red berries in autumn. Rowan is typically found in glens, rocky places and by mountain streams.

Stop 7 **Viewing Point**

In front of you lies the Glenveagh valley, which is 10km long. It is a classic example of a valley that was deepened by a major glacier during the last Ice Age. The glacier occupied a minor gap in the mountains and scoured away the rock beneath it, forming the steep-sided trough or U-shaped valley we see today. It is a textbook example of its kind. The Owenveagh River is clearly too small to have cut such a wide swathe through the mountains. The glacier originated at the head of the valley and flowed northwards towards the Park entrance. It cut deeply into the valley floor. The cliffs are up to 200m high, while Lough Veagh is 49m deep at its deepest point.

As the Ice Age drew to a close, the valley glacier retreated in stages. At each stage, the melting snout of the glacier deposited debris of rocks, gravel and sand in a transverse mound known as a glacial moraine. One moraine spans the valley at the Visitor Centre. It extends into Derrylahan, where a tall plantation of Scots pines grows on the free-draining soil covering the glacial debris. A later moraine, including an outwash fan, which is a fan of sand and gravel deposited by meltwater from the snout of a glacier, spans the valley below Astelleen waterfall.

The steep, rocky slopes of the main glen and Glenlack support small stands of natural oakwood. They are surviving remnants of great oak forests which became established throughout Donegal about 8,000 years ago. Human activities such as tree-felling and stocking with animals greatly reduced their area. Most of the surviving oakwoods in Glenveagh are found on steep slopes and several small remnants can be seen to occupy ravines. The bracken, visible on the opposite slopes, roughly corresponds to formerly wooded ground.

Directly across the lake from the Castle is Sruhanacullia Wood, which is fenced to exclude deer. As can be seen, this has encouraged new growth of heather and trees within the exclosure. The Sruhanacullia stream follows an unusual diagonal route as it flows down to the lake. Close examination reveals that its route is dictated by the walls of a diagonal gully. The gully represents a fracture in the bed-rock, caused by an ancient uplift of the Earth's rock crust.

Notice the narrow drainage ditches high on the opposite slopes. They were dug in a drainage scheme which offered relief work to starving labourers during the Great Potato Famine which started in 1845. These drainage ditches are now overgrown.

Stop 8 **Peat Bog**

At this stop the trail crosses a patch of blanket bog lying in a hillside depression. The hollow is filled with peat to a depth of 1.5 metres. Blanket bog began to spread across Glenveagh over 4,000 years ago. It gradually replaced the pine and birch forests which had covered the slopes (to an altitude of 365m). Tree-felling by early communities probably triggered the spread of blanket bog, though a deterioration in the weather has also been suggested.

Stop 9 **Pineapple Column**

The decorative column on your right is topped with a stone carving of a pineapple. At one time, pineapple was such a luxury that it was widely expressed as an ornamental motif.

At this point, the trail joins the Garden Tour, which leads back to the Castle and the bus park. In summer, refreshments are available at the Castle tea rooms. If you sit outside, you can watch chaffinches searching for crumbs by the tables. They are quite accustomed to humans!

Pineapple column

The Lough Inshagh Walk

This walk leads from the Glen road to the Glebe House and Gallery, situated just east of the Park. The walk follows a cart track leading from Glenveagh Castle to Gartan and Churchhill. It begins at Stop 7 on the Lakeside Walk. The walk passes above scenic Lough Inshagh and offers excellent views of the eastern side of the National Park. Red deer are frequently seen, especially in winter.

Length:　　　　　7km
Time required:　Approx. 1½ hrs.
Surface/gradient: A stony dirt track for most of its length, ending on a quiet tarred road. A moderate climb of 100m in the first 3km, but descending or flat from there on.

Stop 1 Pernettya Shrub
The small-leaved shrub growing densely by the roadside is called *Pernettya* or prickly heath and is particularly common in this part of Glenveagh. It is a garden escape which shows a preference for well-drained roadsides. As deer do not care to graze it, there is a danger it might become a pest in the Park and its rate of spread is therefore being monitored closely.

Stop 2 Whins
The whin, with richly-scented golden flowers, is known as furze or gorse further south in Ireland. It grows in profusion here, where it finds the dry sandy conditions by the roadside to its liking. However, it tends to be killed by frost in severe winters. Despite its prickly leaves, the whin is feasted on by deer in winter, when grazing is otherwise poor.

The green hairstreak butterfly, whose caterpillars feed on the flower petals of the whin, sometimes appears in large numbers along this walk in June. It is quite local in distribution in Ireland and shows a preference for boggy heaths.

The Whin or Gorse flower and leaves

Holly, which deer find even more palatable, is also heavily grazed in winter and any accessible holly trees you see on this walk are likely to be very stunted.

Stop 3 **Mountain Panorama**

From this point, there is a good view of the Derryveagh mountains behind you. The highest peak is Dooish (from the Irish *Dubhais*, meaning black ridge), rising 655m above Lough Veagh. Glaciation and erosion has weathered the granite bed-rock of the mountains, leaving them with smoothly rounded summits. The angular but flat-topped mountain to the north-west is called Muckish. It is composed of a hard rock called quartzite, which better withstands the effects of weathering.

Stop 4 **Rutting Grounds**

The boggy flats below the road are favoured by some of the Park's red deer during the mating season or 'rut', which peaks in October. A dominant stag will gather as many hinds into his harem as he can keep from the attentions of challengers. The mating act is very rarely observed.

Western blanket bog is found on either side of the road. It is covered in specialised plants that survive on limited supplies of nutrients. The sundew and butterwort, for example, feed on insects which they trap on their sticky leaves.

Stop 5 **Lough Inshagh**

Lough Inshagh (from the Irish *Loch Inseach,* meaning lake of islands) is a shallow mountain lake with a good deal of emergent vegetation and wooded islets. The small valley in the mountainside beyond Lough Inshagh was once inhabited by a farming family called Gallagher. The remains of their stone cottage and the fields they tilled can still be seen. The site, surrounded on all sides by uninhabited mountains, is utterly remote and tranquil; very few people live in such an environment today.

In winter, a small herd of whooper swans is usually in residence on the lough. The swans remain until late April, when they return to their breeding grounds in Iceland, though pairs have been known to summer here. There are usually some mallard and teal on the lake in summer.

Otters are occasionally seen on Lough Inshagh and their whistle-like calls are often the first indication of their presence. With luck, you may see one swimming in the lake or climbing onto boulders on the shore.

Sandpiper

The lakeshore, on which there is a small boat-house, has ideal nesting habitat for the common sandpiper, whose sharp piping call gives it away instantly. The sandpiper migrates to Ireland from Africa every year and nests mainly in western counties.

The relatively dry rocky slopes above the road are covered in heather, whose purple blossoms enliven the landscape in season. This is a good place to see wheatears in summer and snow buntings in winter. Other birds you are likely to see include kestrel, stonechat and whinchat. The stonechat is a resident species, while the closely related whinchat migrates between Ireland and Africa. The whinchat is quite local in distribution in Ireland.

Stop 6 **Turf Banks**
Estate workers had turf-cutting rights on the bogland here inside the deer fence, and the turf banks were worked until recent years. The turf-cuttings are relatively well-drained and support good stands of heather. They are gradually returning to nature.

Note: If you do not have transport awaiting you at the Glebe Gallery, then this is a good point at which to turn and retrace your steps to the Visitor Centre. It is a further 3.5km to the Glebe Gallery, though the walk is all downhill from here.

Stop 7 **Gartan View**
From this point, there is a good view of the district of Gartan on the eastern edge of the Park, and of the distant Blue Stack Mountains. There is an extensive plantation of sitka spruce bordering the deer fence. As it matures, the plantation will attract a variety of birds which are currently quite scarce in the Park, such as siskins, coal tits and crossbills. The small lake below you is called Claggan Lough.

Stop 8 **Gate Lodge**
This gate lodge is one of two which guarded the eastern edge of the Glenveagh estate in Mrs. Adair's time. You can make a slight detour at this point to visit Lacknacoo (from the Irish *Leac na Cumha,* meaning flagstone of

GLENVEAGH
NATIONAL
PARK

Aran
Island

Burt Castle

Dert

132

home-sickness), which is some 200 metres away to the right. It is a large stone flag which is reputed to have been the birthplace of Saint Columcille, the famous missionary who was born in Gartan in 521 AD. Cornelia Adair erected the High Cross beside it. Follow the road downhill to join a public road by Lough Nacally. There is a second gate lodge at the junction.

Stone flag and High Cross

Stop 9 **Lough Nacally**

You are now in the district of Gartan, which differs markedly from the Park interior in that it is mostly arable land. Unlike the Park, which has remained mostly uninhabited, Gartan has been settled for at least two thousand years.

Lough Nacally is more productive than the lakes within the National Park. There are substantial reedbeds surrounding it and its bird life is correspondingly richer and more diverse. The birds include breeding dabchicks (little grebes), sedge warblers and water rails. Pochard, teal and tufted duck occur in winter.

The way to the Glebe Gallery is well-signposted from here. En route, you pass along a causeway road between the lakes of Gartan, Nacally and Akibbon. The three lakes were originally one but are now separated by a substantial fen. The fen has mostly become bog, but at the edge of Lough Akibbon there remains an area of fen carr, that is, fen with trees. Lough Akibbon is regularly visited by red-throated divers in summer.

The high ground on which the Glebe is situated was once called Bridge Island, a reference to its formerly more watery surroundings.

The Glebe Gallery, where the Lough Inshagh Walk ends, is owned and run by the National Monuments and Historic Properties Service. It is open for nine days at Easter and from late May to the end of September. You might like to rest and have coffee here before moving on.

Lough Nacally

The Place-Names of the Glenveagh District

Most of Glenveagh's woods, rivers, mountains and lakes have beautifully descriptive Irish names providing an insight into the culture and way of life of past generations. However, in most instances only anglicised versions of the original names appear on Ordnance Survey maps, and their meaning is often obscure.

The process of rendering Irish names into phonetic English began with the Down Survey of the 1650's and was completed by the Ordnance Survey in the 19th century. The place-names were frequently misrepresented, but the English spellings enjoyed sole legal usage from the 1600's until 1922.

North-west Donegal was entirely Irish-speaking up to the mid 19th century and some districts west of Glenveagh are Irish-speaking to this day. However, as the use of Irish declined and areas became depopulated through emigration, many names fell out of use or survived only in phonetic form, and their meaning was lost to many.

Using residual local knowledge and local history and folklore studies, it has been possible to translate the majority of Glenveagh's mapped place-names, and a few of the unmapped. In general, the names are based on features of the natural landscape, described in terms of their physical appearance, their plant and animal life or their usage in farming. Man-made features such as forts, churches and fords lent their names to many sites, and historic or mythological associations were frequently invoked. The area is comprehensively named, harking back to a time when it was densely populated and every patch of ground was valued for its use.

The translations below were supplied by Mr. McGiolla-Easpig of the Ordnance Survey to whom we are very grateful. These translations are the "official" ones of the Ordnance Survey and it is possible that local knowledge may yield further information. The place-names are often quite lyrical, even where their meaning is more mundane. To this day, many are pronounced using the sounds and cadences of the Irish language. The village of

Creeslough, for example, is pronounced *'Creesla'* much as in its Irish name, *An Craoslach,* meaning *'the gorge'*. The *'lough'* in Creeslough is an error perpetuated by successive Ordnance Survey editions, though now official.

Such is the antiquity of the names that many of their stock words - including *doire, leac* (as in slopes) and *mìn* - are no longer part of the Irish vernacular. It may be significant that four of the names whose derivations are still unknown belong to rivers - the Bullaba, Calabber, Clady and Leannan. This suggests that the rivers' names are relatively ancient, maybe because rivers are subject to little change over the centuries, in contrast to the farming environment.

The place-names of Glenveagh National Park, together with prominent place-names in the vicinity of the Park, in their English and Irish versions, together with their meanings, are listed on the following page.

GLENVEAGH
NATIONAL
PARK

Aran
Island

Burt Castle

Derr

English	Irish	Meaning
Altacloghan	Alt a'Chlocháin	Steep glen of the stepping stones
Alteana	Alt Eidhneach	Ivied glen
Ardandun	An tArdán Donn	The brown height
Ardaturr	Ard an Toir	The height of the tall rock
Arduns	An tArd Donn	The brown height
Astelleen	Eas Teilín	The waterfall of 'teilín'
Attinadague	Allt na dTadhg	The steep glen of the Tadhgs
Ballaghgeeha	Bealach Gaoithe	Windy pass
Ballymastocker	Baile Mhic Stocair	The townland of Mac Stocair
Barnes	Bearnas (Bearna)	The gap
Bingorms	Na Beanna Gorma	The blue cliffs
Binnaneane	Binn na nÉan	The cliff of the birds
Binwore	An Bhinn Mhór	The big cliff
Brockagh	Na Brocacha	The badger setts
Bullaba River	Abhainn Bholba	The river of 'bolba'
Bunnatreesruhan	Bun na dTrí Sruthán	Bottom of the three streams
Calabber River	Abhainn Challabair	The river of 'callabar' (poss. meaning: hazel marsh)
Carrickadivean	Carraig an Duibhéin	The rock of the cormorant
Casheltown.	Baile an Chaisil	The town of the stone fort
Creeslough	An Craoslach	The gorge
Claggan Lough	Loch an Chloiginn	The lake of the skull
Croaghlughoge	Cruach Luchóige	Hill of the mouse
Croaghnagapple	Cruach na gCapall	Hill of the horses
Croaghnambrock	Cruach na mBroc	Hill of the badgers
Croaghnanamph	Cruach na nDamh	Hill of the oxen
Croaghnasaggart	Cruach na Sagart	Hill of the priests
Crockballaghgeeha	Cnoc Bhealach Gaoithe	Hill of the windy pass
Crockbrack	An Cnoc Breac	The speckled hill
Crockfadda	An Cnoc Fada	The long hill
Crockmore	An Cnoc Mór	The big hill
Crocknafarragh	Cnoc na bhFaircheach	The hill of the watchers
Crocknageeha	Cnoc na Gaoithe	The hill of the wind
Crocknalaragagh	(Cnoc) Na Leargacha	The slopes
Crocknasharragh	Cnoc na Searrach	Hill of the foals
Crolly	Croithlí	Shaking bog

English	Irish	Meaning
Croloughan	Cró an Locháin	The hollow of the lake
Cronanny Burn	Abhainn Chró Nimhe	The river of the poisoned glen
Crovehy	Cró Bheithe	Hollow of birch
Cummeen	An Coimín	The commonage
Cung	An Chuing	The narrow
Derrybeg	Doire Bheag	Small (oak)wood
Derrylahan	Doire Leathan	Broad (oak)wood
Derryveagh	Doire Bheatha	Woodland of birch
Devlin	Duibhlinn	Black glen or valley
	(ie dubh+gleann)	(orig. Duibhghlinn)
Doochary	An Dúchoraidh	The black weir
	(ie dubh+coraidh)	
Dooish	An Dubhais	The black back or ridge
	(ie dubh+ais)	
Drumnacarry	Droim na Coradh	The ridge of the weir
Drumnalifferny	Droim na Luifearnaí	The ridge of the weeds
Drumnawooa	Droim na bhFuath	The ridge of the spectres
Drumsallagh	Droim Salach	Dirty ridge
Dunlewy	Dún Lúiche	Fort of Lughaidh (Lámhfhada)
		(ie Lughaidh of the Long Arm; myth)
Edenadooish	Éadan na Dubhaise	The face of Dubhais (black ridge)
Errigal	An Earagail	The oratory (-shaped hill)
Garman	Garmán	The ridge
Gartan	Gartán	Small field
Glaskeelan	Glais Chaoláin	Stream of the creek
Glencolumbkille	Gleann Cholm Cille	Colmcille's glen
Glenbeagh	Gleann Bheatha	Glen of birch
Glendowan	Gleann Domhain	Deep glen
Glenlack	Gleann Leac	Glen of the slopes
Glenveagh	Gleann Bheatha	Glen of birch
Gweebarra	Gaoth Beara	Inlet of the river Bior
		(Bior: orig. name of Gweebarra River)

English	Irish	Meaning
Gweedore	Gaoth Dobhair	Inlet of the river Dobhar (Dobhar: orig. name of Gweedore/Crolly River)
Illannaweelane	Oileán na bhFaoileann	The island of the seagulls
Keamnacally	Céim na Caillí	Step of the hag
Kilmacrenan	Cill Mhac nÉanáin	The church of the sons of Éanán
Kingarrow	An Cionn Garbh	The rough headland or hill
Kinnaveagh	Cionn an Bheithe	Headland (or hill) of the birch
Lacknacoo	Leac na Cumha	Flagstone of the homesickness
Leahanmore	An Liathán Mór	The trowel-shaped hill/the grey hill
Leannan River	An Leanainn	(unknown)
Letterkenny	Leitir Ceanainn (ie ceann+fhionn)	The white-topped hillside
Loughanure	Loch an Iúir	Lake of the yew
Losset	An Losaid	The kneading trough (ie hollow)
Lough Agannav	Loch an Ghainnimh	Lake of the sand
Lough Akibbon	Loch Mhic Ciabáin	Lake of Mac Ciabáin
Lough Aleahan	Loch a'Liatháin	Lake of the trowel/lake of the grey hill
Lough Altan	Loch Altáin	Lake of the steep glen
Lough Anlug	Loch an Log	Lake of the hollow
Lough Barra	Loch Beara	Lake of the river Bior (see Gweebarra)
Lough Beg	Loch Beag	Small lake
Lough Inshagh	Loch Inseach	Lake of islands
Lough Meeltoge	Loch Míoltóg	Lake of midges
Lough Nacally	Loch na Caillí	Lake of the hag
Lough Nacung	Loch na Cúng	Lake of the narrows
Lough Nadourcon	Loch na Dobharcon	Lake of the otter
Lough Nambraddan	Loch na mBradán	Lake of the salmon
Lough Naweeloge	Loch na bhFaoileog	Lake of the seagulls
Lough Sallagh	Loch Salach	Dirty lake
Lough Veagh	Loch Bheatha	Lake of the birchwood
Maghernashangan	Machaire na Seangán	Plain of the ants
Maumlack	Mám Leac	Pass of the slopes
Meenadreen	Mín an Droighin	Hill pasture of the blackthorn

English	Irish	Meaning
Meenaneagh	*Mín an Fhia*	Hill pasture of the deer
Meenashammer	*Mín na Seamar*	Hill pasture of the clover
Meenbog	*An Mhín Bhog*	The soft hill pasture
Meennamolt	*Mín na Molt*	Hill pasture of the wethers
Meensnee	*Mín na Sní*	Hill pasture of the flow
Moylenanav	*Maol na nDamh*	Bare hilltop of the oxen
Muckish	*An Mhucais (ie muc+ais)*	Pig-backed hill
Mullangore	*Maolán na nGabhar*	Bare hilltop of the goats
Owenacally	*Abhainn na Caillí*	River of the hag
Owenbeg	*An Abhainn Bheag*	The small river
Owencarrow	*Abhainn Choradh*	River of (the) weir(s)
Pollgarriv	*An Poll Garbh*	The rough hole
Saggartnadooish	*Sagairt na Dubhaise*	The priest of An Dubhais
Slieve Snaght	*Sliabh Sneachta*	Mountain of (the) snow
Sranaglogh	*Srath na gCloch*	River-meadow of the stones
Sruhanacullia	*Sruthán na Coille*	Stream of the wood
Sturricknagower	*Storraic na nGabhar*	The peak or prominence of the goats
Termon	*An Tearmann*	The sanctuary (lands a third)

Aran
Island

GLENVEAGH
NATIONAL
PARK

Kamelton

Burt Castle

Derry

140

The Birds of Glenveagh National Park

S: Summer   W: Winter   V: Vagrant

Red-throated diver	S:	*Gavia stellata*	❏
Black-throated diver	V:	*Gavia arctica*	❏
Little grebe (dabchick)	S:	*Tachybaptus ruficollis*	❏
Great crested grebe	S:	*Podiceps cristatus*	❏
Cormorant	S/W:	*Phalacrocorax carbo*	❏
Heron	S/W:	*Ardea cinerea*	❏
White stork	V:	*Ciconia ciconia*	❏
Mute swan	S/W:	*Cygnus olor*	❏
Whooper swan	W:	*Cygnus cygnus*	❏
Greenland white-fronted goose	W:	*Anser albifrons flavirostris*	❏
Shelduck	V:	*Tadorna tadorna*	❏
Mallard	S/W:	*Anas platyrhynchos*	❏
Teal	S/W:	*Anas crecca*	❏
Pochard	W:	*Aythya ferina*	❏
Tufted duck	W:	*Aythya fuligula*	❏
Goldeneye	W:	*Bucephala clangula*	❏
Merganser (red-breasted)	S:	*Mergus serrator*	❏
Goosander	S/W:	*Mergus merganser*	❏
Osprey	V:	*Pandion haliaetus*	❏
Sparrowhawk	S/W:	*Accipiter nisus*	❏
Buzzard	V:	*Buteo buteo*	❏
Golden eagle	V:	*Aquila chrysaetos*	❏
Hen harrier	V:	*Circus cyaneus*	❏
Peregrine falcon	S/W:	*Falco peregrinus*	❏
Merlin	S/W:	*Falco columbarius*	❏
Kestrel	S/W:	*Falco tinnunculus*	❏
Red grouse	S/W:	*Lagopus lagopus*	❏
Red-legged Partridge	V:	*Alectoris rufa*	❏
Pheasant	S/W:	*Phasianus colchicus*	❏
Water rail	S/W:	*Rallus aquaticus*	❏
Moorhen	S/W:	*Gallinula chloropus*	❏
Coot	S/W:	*Fulica atra*	❏
OysterCatcher	V:	*Haematopus ostragelegus*	❏
Ringed Plover	V:	*Charadrius hiaticula*	❏

Birds continued

Golden Plover	S/W:	*Pluvialis apricaria*	❏
Dunlin	S:	*Calidris alpina*	❏
Common sandpiper	S:	*Actitis hypoleucos*	❏
Curlew	S/W:	*Numenius arquata*	❏
Whimbrel	V:	*Numenius phaeopus*	❏
Woodcock	S/W:	*Scolopax rusticola*	❏
Snipe	S/W:	*Gallinago gallinago*	❏
Jack snipe	W:	*Lymnocryptes minimus*	❏
Great black-backed gull	V:	*Larus marinus*	❏
Lesser black-backed gull	V:	*Larus fuscus*	❏
Common gull	S/W:	*Larus canus*	❏
Woodpigeon	S/W:	*Columba palumbus*	❏
Collared dove	V:	*Streptopelia decaocto*	❏
Cuckoo	S:	*Cuculus canorus*	❏
Long-eared owl	S/W:	*Asio otis*	❏
Short-eared owl	W:	*Asio flammeus*	❏
Swift	S:	*Apus apus*	❏
Kingfisher	V:	*Alcedo atthis*	❏
Skylark	S:	*Alauda arvensis*	❏
Swallow	S:	*Hirundo rustica*	❏
House martin	S:	*Delichon urbica*	❏
Sand martin	V:	*Riparia riparia*	❏
Tree pipit	V:	*Anthus trivialis*	❏
Meadow pipit	S/W:	*Anthus pratensis*	❏
Grey wagtail	S:	*Motacilla cinerea*	❏
Dunnock	S/W:	*Prunella modularis*	❏
Waxwing	V:	*Bombycilla garrulus*	❏
Grasshopper warbler	S:	*Locustella naevia*	❏
Sedge warbler	S:	*Acrocephalus schoenobaenus*	❏
Whitethroat	S:	*Sylvia communis*	❏
Garden Warbler	S:	*Sylvia borin*	❏
Blackcap	S:	*Sylvia atricapilla*	❏
Willow warbler	S:	*Phylloscopus trochilis*	❏
Chiffchaff	S:	*Phylloscopus collybita*	❏
Wood warbler	S:	*Phylloscopus sibilatrix*	❏
Goldcrest	S/W:	*Regulus regulus*	❏

Birds continued

Spotted flycatcher	S/W:	*Muscicapa striata*	❏
Stonechat	S:	*Saxicola torquata*	❏
Whinchat	S:	*Saxicola rubetra*	❏
Wheatear	S:	*Oenanthe oenanthe*	❏
Redstart	S:	*Phoenicurus phoenicurus*	❏
Robin	S/W:	*Erithacus rubecula*	❏
Blackbird	S/W:	*Turdus merula*	❏
Ring ouzel	S:	*Turdus torquatus*	❏
Fieldfare	W:	*Turdus pilaris*	❏
Redwing	W:	*Turdus iliacus*	❏
Song thrush	S/W:	*Turdus philomelos*	❏
Mistle thrush	S/W:	*Turdus viscivorus*	❏
Long-tailed tit	S/W:	*Aegithelos caudatus*	❏
Coal tit	S/W:	*Parus ater*	❏
Blue tit	S/W:	*Parus cyanus*	❏
Great tit	S/W:	*Parus major*	❏
Treecreeper	S/W:	*Certhia familiaris*	❏
Wren	S/W:	*Troglodytes troglodytes*	❏
Dipper	S/W:	*Cinclus cinclus hibernicus*	❏
Yellowhammer	W:	*Emberiza citrinella*	❏
Reed bunting	S/W:	*Emberiza schoeniclus*	❏
Snow bunting	W:	*Plectrophenax nivalis*	❏
Chaffinch	S/W:	*Fringilla coelebs*	❏
Goldfinch	S/W:	*Carduelis carduelis*	❏
Siskin	S/W:	*Carduelis spinus*	❏
Redpoll	S/W:	*Acanthis flammea*	❏
Twite	V:	*Acanthis flavirostris*	❏
Linnet	V:	*Acanthis cannabina*	❏
Greenfinch	S/W:	*Carduelis chloris*	❏
Bullfinch	S/W:	*Pyrrhula pyrrhula*	❏
Crossbill	S/W:	*Loxia curvirostra*	❏
Jay	S/W:	*Garrulus glandarius*	❏
Magpie	S/W:	*Pica pica*	❏
Raven	S/W:	*Corvus corax*	❏
Hooded Crow	S/W:	*Corvus corone corone*	❏
Carrion Crow	V:	*Corvus corone cornix*	❏

The Mammals of Glenveagh National Park

Pygmy shrew	*Sorex minutus*	❏
Daubenton's bat	*Myotis daubentoni*	❏
Whiskered bat	*Selysius mystacinus*	❏
Natterer's bat	*Selysius nattereri*	❏
Pipistrelle	*Pipistrellus pipistrellus*	❏
Leisler's bat	*Nyctalus leisleri*	❏
Hare	*Lepus timidus hibernicus*	❏
Long-tailed field mouse	*Apodemus sylvaticus*	❏
Fox	*Vulpes vulpes*	❏
Pine Marten	*Martes martes*	❏
Stoat	*Mustela erminea hibernica*	❏
Mink	*Mustela vison*	❏
Badger	*Meles meles*	❏
Otter	*Lutra lutra*	❏
Red deer	*Cervus elaphus*	❏

Reptile

Lizard	*Lacerta vivipara*	❏

Amphibian

Frog	*Rana temporaria*	❏

Fish

Eel	*Anguilla anguilla*	❏
Salmon	*Salmo salar*	❏
Sea trout (brown trout)	*Salmo trutta*	❏
Arctic charr	*Salvelinus alpinus*	❏
Three spined stickleback	*Gasterosteus aculeatis*	❏

The Butterflies of Glenveagh National Park

Large White	*Pieris brassicae*	❏
Small White	*Pieris rapae*	❏
Green-veined White	*Pieris napi*	❏
Orange-tip	*Anthocharis cardamines*	❏
Speckled wood	*Pararge aegeria*	❏
Small Copper	*Lycaena phlaeas*	❏
Common Blue	*Polymmatus icarus*	❏
Holly Blue	*Celastrina argiolus*	❏
Red Admiral	*Vanessa atalanta*	❏
Tortoise Shell	*Aglais urticae*	❏
Peacock	*Inachis io*	❏
Dark Green Fritillary	*Argynnis aglaja*	❏
Silver-washed Fritillary	*Argynnis paphia*	❏
Speckled Wood	*Pararge aegeria*	❏
Meadow Brown	*Maniola jurtina*	❏
Small Heath	*Coenonympha pamphilus*	❏
Ringlet	*Aphantopus hyperantus*	❏

Moths (Lepidoptera) of Glenveagh National Park

	Acronicta sp.	❏
Large Ear	*Amphipyra lucens*	❏
Dark Arches	*Apamea monglypha*	❏
Black Rustic	*Apororophyla nigra*	❏
Garden Tiger moth	*Arctia caja*	❏
Small Wainscot	*Arenastola pygmina*	❏
Gold Spangle	*Autographa (Noctua) bractea*	❏
Flame	*Axylia putris*	❏
Peppered moth	*Biston betularia*	❏
Cinnabar	*Callimorhpa jacobaeae*	❏
Antler moth	*Cerapterix graminis*	❏
Lunar Marbled Brown	*Chaonia ruficornis*	❏
Pink Barred Sallow	*Citria lutea*	❏
Feathered Thorn	*Colotois pennaria*	❏
Muslin moth	*Cycnia mendica*	❏
Elephant Hawk-moth	*Deilephila elphenor*	❏
Burnished Brass	*Diachrysia chrysitis*	❏
Clouded Buff	*Diachrysia sannio*	❏
Ingrailed Clay	*Diarsia mendico*	❏
Bright-Line Brown-eye	*Diatoraxia oleracea*	❏
Dark Marbled Carpet	*Dysstroma citrata*	❏
Carpet moth	*Dysstroma concinnata*	❏
Marbled Carpet moth	*Dysstroma truncata*	❏
Common Heath	*Ematurga atomaria*	❏
Canary Shouldered Thorn	*Ennomos alniaria*	❏
White-Line Dart	*Euxoa tritica*	❏
Ear Moth	*Hydraecia oculea*	❏
Poplar Hawk-moth	*Laothoe populi*	❏
Oak Eggar	*Lasiocampa quercus*	❏
Brown-Line Bright-Eye	*Leucania conigera*	❏
Clouded Border	*Lomaspilis marginata*	❏
True Lovers Knot	*Lycophotia porphyrea*	❏
Fox moth	*Macrothylacia rubi*	❏
Smoky Wainscot	*Mythimna impusa*	❏
Large Yellow Underwing	*Noctua pronuba*	❏

Aran Island

GLENVEAGH
NATIONAL
PARK

Burt Castle

Derr

Moths continued

Pebble Prominent	*Notodonta ziczac*	❏
Brown China Mark	*Nyphula nymphaeta*	❏
Flame Shoulder	*Orchropleura plecta*	❏
Hebrew Character	*Orthosia gothica*	❏
Powdered Quaker	*Orthosia gracilis*	❏
Swallow-tailed moth	*Ourapteryx sambucaria*	❏
Wood Tiger moth	*Parasemia plantaginis*	❏
Buff Tip	*Phalera bucephala*	❏
Drinker	*Philudoria potatoria*	❏
Angle Shades	*Phlogophora meticulosa*	❏
Ruby Tiger moth	*Phragmatobia fuliginosa*	❏
Beautiful Golden Y	*Plusia pulchrina*	❏
December Moth	*Poecilocampa populi*	❏
Argent and Sable	*Rhuemaptera hastata*	❏
Early Thorn	*Selinia bilunaria*	❏
Early Thorn	*Selinia dentaria*	❏
Herald	*Scoliopteryx libatrix*	❏
White Ermine	*Spilosoma lubricipeda*	❏
Buff Ermine	*Spilosoma lutea*	❏
	Sterrha sp.	❏
Anomalous	*Stilbia anomala*	❏
Peach Blossom	*Thyatira batis*	❏
Red Sword-grass	*Xylena vetusta*	❏

Dragonflies and damselflies *Odonata*

Common hawker	*Aeshna juncea*	❏
Four-spotted chaser	*Libellula quadrimaculata*	❏
Black darter	*Sympetrum scotticum (danae)*	❏
Common darter	*Sympetrum striolatum*	❏
Banded agrion	*Callopteryx splendens*	❏
Variable damselfly	*Coenagrion puella*	❏
Common blue damselfly	*Enallagma cyathigerum*	❏
Large red damselfly	*Pyrrhosoma nymphula*	❏
Emerald damselfly	*Lestes sponsa*	❏
Common Ischnura	*Ischnura elegans*	❏
	Orthetrum coerulescens	❏

GLENVEAGH
NATIONAL
PARK

Ramelton
Burt Castle
Derry
Aran
Island

The Plants of Glenveagh National Park

Ferns

Athyrium filix-femina
Blechnum spicant
Dryopteris aemula
Dryopteris aemula
Dryopteris borreri

Dryopteris dilitata
Hymenophyllum wilsonii
Osmunda regalis
Polypodium spp.
Polypodium vulgare agg

Pteridium aquilinum
Thelypteris oreopteris
Thelypteris phegopteris
Thelypteris phegopteris
Trichomanes speciosum

Grasses

Agrostis canina
Agrostis stolonifera
Agrostis tenuis
Anthoxanthum odoratum
Brachypodium sylvaticum
Carex binervis
Carex demissa
Carex echinata
Carex flacca
Carex laevigata
Carex lepidocarpa
Carex nigra
Carex pallescens
Carex panicea
Carex pulicaris
Carex remota
Carex rostrata
Carex sylvatica

Cynosurus cristatus
Dactylis glomerata
Danthonia decumbens
Deschampsia flexuosa
Eleocharis multicaulis
Eriophorum angustifolium
Eriophorum vaginatum
Festuca altissima
Festuca gigantea
Festuca ovina
Festuca rubra
Festuca vivipara
Glyceria fluitans
Holcus lanatus
Holcus mollis
Juncus acutifloris
Juncus articulatus
Juncus bufonius

Juncus bulbosis
Juncus conglomeratus
Juncus effusus
Juncus squarrosus
Juncus tenuis
Luzula multiflora
Luzula sylvatica
Milium effusum
Molinia caerulea
Nardus stricta
Phragmites australis
Plantago lanceolata
Poa pratensis
Rhynchospora alba
Schoenus nigricans
Scirpus caespitosis

Dicotyledon Herbs

Ajuga reptans
Anagallis tenella
Anemone nemorosa
Angelica sylvestris
Antennaria dioica
Callitriche stagnalis
Cardamine flexuosa
Cardamine pratensis
Centaurea nigra
Chrysosplenium oppositifolium
Circaea intermedia
Circaea lutetiana
Cirsium dissectum
Cirsium palustre
Conopodium majus
Crepis paludosa
Digitalis purpurea
Drosera anglica
Drosera intermedia
Drosera rotundifolia
Epilobium angustifolium
Epilobium montanum
Epilobium nerterioides
Euphrasia micrantha
Filipendula ulmaria
Frageria vesca
Galium saxatile
Hieracium sp.
Hypericum androsaemum

Hypericum pulchrum
Hypochoeris radicata
Jasione montana
Lathyrus montanus
Leontodon autumnale
Leontodon taraxocoides
Littorella uniflora
Lobelia dortmana
Lotus corniculatus
Lotus uliginosus
Lysimachia nemorum
Lysimachia vulgaris
Melampyrum pratense
Mentha arvensis
Menyanthes trifoliata
Oxalis acetosella
Pedicularis palustris
Pedicularis sylvatica
Pinguicula lusitanica
Pinguicula palustris
Pinguicula vulgaris
Polgonum persicaria
Polygala serpyllifolia
Potentilla anserina
Potentilla erecta
Potentilla sterilis
Primula vulgaris
Prunella vulgaris
Ranunculus acris

Ranunculus ficaria
Ranunculus flammula
Ranunculus repens
Rhinanthus minor
Rhodolia rosa
Rumex acetosa
Rumex acetosella
Sagina procumbens
Sanicula europaea
Saxifraga stellaris
Scrophularia
Senecio aquaticus
Senecio jacobaea
Solidago virgaurea
Stellaria alsine
Succisa pratensis
Taraxacum cf. paludosum
Teucrium scorodonia
Trifolium repens
Umbilicus rupestris
Umbillicus rupestris
Utricularia minor
Veronica chamaedrys
Veronica montana
Veronica officinalis
Vicia cracca
Viola palustre
Viola riviniana

Monocotyledon Herbs

Allium ursinum
Dactylorhiza maculata
Deschampsia caespitosa

Endymion non-scriptus
Listera cordata
Narthecium ossifragum

Trichophorum caespitosum
Orchis mascula
Potomogeton natans

Shrubs and Climbers

Arctostaphyllus uva-ursi

Calluna vulgaris

Empetrum nigrum

Erica cinerea

Erica tetralix

Hedera helix

Juniperis communis var communis

Juniperis communis var nana

Lonicera periclymenum

Myrica gale

Pernettya mucronata

Rhododendron ponticum

Rosa canina

Rosa pimpinellifolia

Rubus fruticosus

Salix herbacea

Salix repens

Ulex europaeus

Vaccinium myrtillus

Vaccinium vitis-idaea

Trees

Abies spp.

Acer pseudoplatanus

Alnus glutinosa

Betula pubescens

Corylus avellana

Crataegus monogyna

Fagus syvatica

Fraxinus excelsior

Ilex aquifolium

Larix decidua

Picea abies

Picea sitchensis

Pinus contorta var latifolia

Pinus nigra

Pinus sylvestris

Populus tremula

Prunus padus

Prunus spinosa

Quercus petraea

Salix aurita

Salix cinerea

Sorbus aucuparia

Sorbus rupicola

Taxus baccata

Tsuga heterophylla

Ulmus glabra

Garden Plants

Acer palmatum 'Atropurpureum'

Acer pseudoplatanus
'Brilliantissimum'

Arbutus x andracnoides

Betula pubescens

Brachyglottis 'Sunshine'

Brachyglottis buchananii

Brachyglottis hectoris

Buxus sempervirens

Cedrus atlantica 'Glauca'

Cercidiphyllum japonicum

Cordyline australis

Cordyline indivisa

Corylus avellana

Cotoneaster horizontalis

Crinodendron hookerianum

Cryptomeria japonica 'Elegans'

Cupressus sempervirens

Dicksonia antarctica

Eleagnus pungens

Embothrium coccineum

Eucryphia cordifolia

Eucryphia moorei

Eucryphia x nymansensis
'Mount Usher'

Fasicularia bicolor

Fothergilla major

Gevuina avellana

Griselinia littoralis

Gunnera manicata

Hoheria lyalli

Hoheria populnea

Hosta sieboldiana 'Elegans'

Hydrangea petiolaris

Ilex aquifolium

Luma apiculata

Luzula sylvatica

Magnolia tripetala

Magnolia wilsonii

Metrosideros umbellata

Michelia doltsopa

Nothofagus cunninghamii

Nothofagus dombeyi

Nothofagus obliqua

Nothofagus procera

Olearia 'Henry Travers'

Olearia macrodonta

Olearia x hastii

Osmanthus heterophyllus
'Myrtifolius'

Osmanthus x burkwoodii

Phormium tenax

Pieris 'Forest Flame'

Pieris formosa 'Wakehurst'

Pinus nigra

Pinus sylvestris

Podocarpus salignus

Prunus padus

Pseodopanax ferox

Pseudopanax crassifolius

Pseudowintera colorata

Quercus petraea

Rhododendron 'Mulroy
Vanguard'

Rhododendron 'Shilsonii'

Rhododendron arboreum

Rhododendron cinnabarinum

Rhododendron falconeri

Rhododendron johnstoneanum

Rhododendron lindleyi

Rhododendron macabeanum

Rhododendron megacalyx

Rhododendron mollyanum

Rhododendron ponticum

Rhododendron protistum

Rhododendron sinogrande

Rhododendron yakushimanum

Stuartia koreana

Styrax japonica

Trachycarpus fortunei

GLENVEAGH
NATIONAL
PARK

Aran
Island

■ Burt Castle

Derry

Further Reading

The History of Glenveagh

Dolan L.   Land War and Eviction in Derryveagh 1840-1865.
                                    Annaverna Press Dundalk. 1980.
Gavan Duffy C.   My Life in Two Hemispheres. First publ. 1898,
                                    reprinted Irish University Press, Dublin. 1969.
McClain M.G.   The Rebellion of Sir Cahir O'Doherty and its Influence on
                                    the Ulster Plantation. University of Philadelphia. 1930.
McCracken E.   The Irish Woods since Tudor Times.
                                    David and Charles, London. 1971.
O'Keeffe C.   The History of Glenveagh. OPW, Dublin. 1991.
Simms J.G.   Donegal in the Ulster Plantations.
                                    Irish Geography 6:386-393. 1972.
Vaughan W.E.   Sin, Sheep and Scotsmen - John George Adair and the
                                    Derryveagh Evictions 1861. Appletree Press, Belfast. 1981.

Glenveagh Castle

Beckwith J.   Kingsley Porter - Blazing the Trail in Europe.
                                    Apollo, Dec. 1970
Burton H. T.   A History of the JA Ranch. Austin, Texas. 1928
Guinness D. & J. O'Brien   Great Irish Houses and Castles. London. 1992.
Guinness D. & W. Ryan   Irish Houses and Castles. London. 1971

Rishel J.J.   The Henry P. McIlhenny Collection.
                                    Philadelphia Museum of Art. 1987

Glenveagh Gardens

Brown J.   Lanning Roper and his Gardens. Rizzoli, New York , 1987.
Craig A. J.   Glenveagh Gardens. OPW, Dublin. 1991
George M. & P.Bowe   The Gardens of Ireland. New York Graphic Society. 1986

Geology

Pitcher W.F.   The Geology of Donegal: A Study of Granite Emplacement
                                    and Un-Roofing. Wiley InterScience. 1972.

Scientific Studies and Articles

A number of scientific studies about the plant and animal life and the physical features of Glenveagh National Park have been undertaken since the 1970's. Details on these are available on request from the Park Administration Office.